BODY BEFORE

SPORTS PERFORMANCE FOR CHEERLEADING

by Jessica Zoo

CONTRIBUTORS

Matthew Goldberg - Editor

Elise Wilson - Technical Editor

Jeff Benson - Sports Psychology

Debbie Love - Education Specialist

Rachel Berenson-Perkins - Education Specialist

Tristram Newnham - Kinesiology

Coach Sahil M - Nutrition

Corey Stone - Illustrator

Published by Cheerobics®

3801 N Capital of Texas Hwy

E-240, Austin, TX 78746

www.cheerobics.net

I HAVE NO SPECIAL TALENT. I AM ONLY PASSIONATELY CURIOUS.

- ALBERT EINSTEIN -

DISCLAIMER

THE INFORMATION SHARED IN THIS BOOK IS DESIGNED TO
PROVIDE HELPFUL INSIGHTS INTO THE SUBJECTS DISCUSSED.
THIS BOOK IS NOT MEANT TO BE USED, NOR SHOULD IT BE USED
AS A REPLACEMENT FOR PROFESSIONAL COACHING OR FITNESS
INSTRUCTION. IN THE CASE OF A NEED FOR ANY SUCH
EXPERTISE CONSULT WITH THE APPROPRIATE PROFESSIONAL.

THIS BOOK DOES NOT CONTAIN ALL INFORMATION
AVAILABLE ON THE SUBJECT. THIS BOOK HAS NOT BEEN
CREATED TO BE SPECIFIC TO ANY INDIVIDUAL OR
ORGANISATIONAL SITUATIONS OR NEEDS.

EVERY EFFORT HAS BEEN MADE TO MAKE THIS BOOK AS
ACCURATE AS POSSIBLE. THERE MAY, HOWEVER, BE
TYPOGRAPHICAL AND/OR CONTENT ERRORS. THEREFORE, THIS
BOOK SHOULD SERVE ONLY AS A GENERAL GUIDE AND NOT AS
THE ULTIMATE SOURCE OF SUBJECT INFORMATION.

REFERENCES ARE PROVIDED FOR INFORMATIONAL PURPOSES
ONLY AND DO NOT CONSTITUTE ENDORSEMENT OF ANY
WEBSITE OR ANY OTHER SOURCES. THE AUTHOR AND
PUBLISHER SHALL HAVE NO LIABILITY OR RESPONSIBILITY TO
ANY PERSON OR ENTITY REGARDING ANY LOSS OR DAMAGE
INCURRED, DIRECTLY OR INDIRECTLY, BY THE INFORMATION
CONTAINED IN THIS BOOK.

CONTENTS

1

INTRODUCTION

Being a cheerleading coach is one of the most wonderful and rewarding jobs in the world. Nothing beats the smile on an athlete's face when he or she successfully performs a new skill for the very first time, or when a team achieves a goal they've been working toward under your tutelage. It is a role that comes with many responsibilities including the welfare, development and safety of your athletes. A coach is required to have a myriad of different qualities and skills. They should be inspirational, creative, respectful, qualified, passionate, diplomatic, persevering, determined, flexible, approachable, knowledgeable, organised, encouraging, and self-assured. Just to name just a few.

If you think about it, the concept of competitive cheerleading is fairly odd: a pastime that was primarily conceived as a sideline activity to support "real sport" teams on campus has evolved into a whole sport of its own. Competitive cheerleading left the sidelines a long time ago and it has evolved so much since its primitive form that it's barely recognisable. Now, all-star and competitive cheer is more comparable to group gymnastics than anything else.

The past decade shows us that we have grown exponentially, emerging from a sport where only top athletes could compete, into a worldwide industry accessible to all ages and ability levels. This rapid growth has brought our community many advantages, and some unexpected challenges too. Advancements in individual skills and organisational expectations have outpaced education, technique and safety as we have tried to manage the increasing volume of athletes, teams and competitions.

It's clear to see we're in a sport where the demands on the body are just as high as they are in gymnastics. However, many of the professionals in our industry have an understanding of the body that is far inferior to fitness instructors for example, who are just teaching basic squats, pushups and grapevines as opposed to teaching people how to fling each other through the air.

We shouldn't, however, see this lack of basics in our education system as a failure. Cheerleading was never designed to be a sport in the first place: it evolved. Cheerleading did not start with "let's train bodies for acrobatic sport" as a concept. It started with "let's promote school spirit" and then became "let's get the most athletic kids in school to throw impressive visual routines for our pep rallies and games." Now we go as far as finding ourselves watching at the world championships among a sea of people outside the arena, clambering at the gates of a stadium filled to capacity. The concept of "people cheering cheerleaders" baffles those outside our industry. We are an army of bows. We ARE a sport. Statistically, the most dangerous sport. But how did we get here?

The fact that cheerleading has grown into a competitive sport was not premeditated. Once it hit a tipping point, we'd all become more preoccupied with keeping up with the demands of the exponential growth: How do we stay one step ahead of other teams? How do we give athletes and their parents what they need while we keep doing our jobs? How does the cheerleading gym business model even work? How can we make this sustainable? How can we grow our teams? The concept of training 'acrobatic' cheerleaders from scratch, regardless of their athletic past, is relatively new. It's one of the first questions that should be asked, and finally, it is slowly being answered.

Coaching cheerleading has been a job learned through many hours of apprenticeships in contrast to strict qualification routes (compared to fitness or gymnastics, for example) Understanding how our sport evolved allows us to accept the fact that kinesiology, fitness and sports science have been overlooked in the past, but it's never too late to include these concepts as part of the future of competitive cheerleading.

I fell in love with cheerleading at a late age (close to retirement years by USA standards) and quickly crossed over to coaching where I felt the fit was best for me. Even at a grassroots level, I have always seen cheer as a sport no matter what other's views have been. My passion has always been about team transformation. I remember asking myself from the start "How can I take what I have and push the boundaries? How can we make the best of what we have? How can we make this journey something we will all remember and be proud of, regardless of where we are placed?" For me, it's always been about 'the climb'. It's been about digging deep into being the best you can be at the sport you love, regardless of your natural ability.

Originally, when I set out to create Cheerobics® Fitness it was designed to bring the joy of cheerleading to those who wanted to unleash their inner cheerleader through a fun but challenging fitness program. At the time I started with the Cheerobics® concept, I was still coaching cheer. It was only once I started to get a deeper understanding of fitness that I realised how much our sport has been missing out. After this awakening I set out to create the INTENSITY™ method (the Cheerobics® branch dedicated to athletic development) so that I could help coaches and cheerleaders get the same insight that I had found. I knew they needed to see cheerleading through the fitness looking glass: to visualise the bigger picture of the sport and build solid foundations through the body before pushing the skill.

I may not have been the most natural gymnast from the get-go, but the hurdles I faced forced me to understand how I could use my body to its best advantage. It was my physical limitations, passion for fitness and unquenchable thirst to leave no stone unturned, explore all the elements of every cheerleading skill and how to train the body to achieve them. This was my mission for *Body Before Skill*: to research, test and bring together all of the best knowledge available on cheerleading, sports science and conditioning to bring together one resource that we could all use as coaches.

Coaching also comes with its own challenges which are difficult for others to understand. People rarely take into consideration the personnel, financial implications, logistics, pressures, obligations, and more that shape the decisions coaches make. It is hard (or, more honestly, impossible) to keep everyone happy, especially when it comes to parents, participants and/or coaching peers. At times it can feel like a battle to get everyone to agree and accept the decision. If you're firm, people think you're stubborn. If you listen to everyone, you're indecisive! But no matter what, and as odd as it might sound to the external world: cheer is a vocation. Cheer coaches persevere through adverse conditions because we are dedicated to our mission. We've been bitten by the cheer bug and that's a condition for life.

I truly hope that *Body Before Skill* gives you the same 'AHA' moments that I had when researching and putting my learning into practice. I hope it will help you understand the skill and athlete development in more detail, giving you that little bit of extra insight into what our bodies go through when we train for and compete in the sport of cheer. Hopefully, at the end of the metaphorical rainbow, you will also find a pot of gold.

Or a championship ring.

ACKNOWLEDGEMENTS

This book would not have been possible without some key people who I wanted to thank, who have vastly contributed to this journey.

Debbie Love, my greatest inspiration in the cheerleading industry who unknowingly showed me the path I wanted to take. Thank you for taking the time and giving me your support on this mission.

Sahil M. and Jeff Benson: it's been an absolute pleasure working with you; I thank you for being so generous with your expertise and precious contributions. Tristram Newnham, for being my translator and tutor in wonderful world of biomechanics. Thanks for your dedicated patience.

Elise Wilson: by the time this goes to publication, only you and I really know what it means when we decide to go down a rabbit hole. Thank you for going far beyond your job description in everything you do and for truly setting the standard for what loyalty and dedication truly means in the workplace.

Matt Goldberg: you have shown me what it means to be a phoenix. Thank you for your persistence and your ability to rip this book to shreds so that it could be the best version it could be. 'No pain, no gain' may not be the right philosophy for training athletes but it certainly worked in shaping *Body Before Skill*.

My teachers: Mr. Brown, for teaching me to adopt English as my native language and how to love writing. Mr. Greenway, for sharing your passion for Biology which so strongly influenced my curiosity towards sports science; but mostly for showing me academic aptitude and grades are not the only thing that makes a good student.

Rachel Berenson-Perkins, a wonderful coach and friend who has been up with me since the Jurassic years at university, geeking out on cheerleading and always being there to bounce ideas around until the wee hours of the morning.

Lars: my partner in life and crime, for feeding me, being there to bounce ideas off, keeping me alive and being amazing at dealing with the work-zombie version of me during this epic journey!

Finally, to all the coaches and athletes who have been encouraging and inspired me on the *Body Before Skill* journey.

FOREWORD BY DEBBIE LOVE

This sport of cheerleading is still very young, but I have been involved cheering since 1965 and doing gymnastics as well as track from middle school through college at Memphis State University, so I have watched it evolve from infancy to young adulthood. At first, the physical demands were your vocal cords, sharp motions and a great deal of enthusiasm. Soon we started doing stunts, jumps and basket tosses with tumbling growing more difficult by the year. With jumps being introduced, we added an element that recruits more muscles than any other skill making our bodies cry for proper training.

Cheerleading began in the late 1800s with yell squads for football games just doing chants and sideline activities. It was basically made up of young men. November 2, 1898 was the year of the first yell squad. Its evolvement included going through the war era where it became more female-dominant, tumbling and megaphones were beginning to be used. Subsequently in 1948 Lawrence Herkimer from Southern Methodist University started NCA and began running clinics. Cheerleading next began to be seen in high schools and today 80% of public schools in the USA have cheerleaders with the majority of the athletes being between the ages of 12-17.

In 1972, professional cheerleading organisations started and Title IX, an amendment to the USA Constitution requiring schools to provide equitable athletic participation opportunities for its female and male students came into effect. In 1976, the liberty stunt was invented and in 1979 the first basket toss was created by UCA. By 1987 the first all-star teams were competing at NCA and in 2004 the USASF hosted the first Worlds competition. Today we have numerous all-star gyms with some numbering into the thousands of athletes, and becoming an extremely popular activity internationally.

Our conditioning needs have grown astronomically; however, the average coach's knowledge about the body and expertise in conditioning their athletes appropriately has not grown relative to the demands of the body. This has created major problems with both new and overuse injuries. There is much education out there on injury prevention and conditioning and recovery for the body. However, because we have been overly concerned with just putting skills on the floor, and our eyes fixated on that almighty trophy we have collectively neglected being responsible coaches.

We have practices without warmup. We have no time for a well-structured practice because we have to get those skills. We have back-to-back-to-back practices without regard for proper recovery time for our athletes' bodies. For many years now, we have been building skills on deficient bodies, and this is neither smart nor responsible.

As coaches, we must accept responsibility for training both our minds and our bodies for the skills we are teaching. The idea of 'no pain, no gain' gained popularity a few years back and is the furthermost from the truth. Maybe a little soreness is normal but pain is not a requirement for a sport. It is a consequence of ignorance in the area of preparing our body for athleticism.

In the late 90s we were given the facts that no longer should we do static stretches at the beginning of practice because it reduced our explosiveness. We now know we should begin our practices with a dynamic full range of motion warm-up. However, people still include static stretches such as splits for a minute or more in their pre-practice warm up. In the past few years, we have found the need for athlete assessment and pre-participation physicals as well as learning that we need to maintain the integrity of the core while our centre of gravity is moving through the air as in tumbling, stunting, pyramids and basket tosses: not just train core stabilisation when we are still. All of this adds up to an extreme demand for knowledge in how to keep our athletes fit in order to reduce the risk of injury. It is imperative that every coach who deals with cheerleaders learns how to produce a fit athlete who can remain almost injury free for their whole career, which may span from age 3-22 and beyond.

I have read and digested *Body Before Skill* and the complete INTENSITY™ programme and can say with complete authority that it is a programme that will produce fit athletes as well as smart coaches who see the whole athlete and not just their skills.

The mental aspect of cheerleading is more important than the physical in that it comprises 90% of what we do. Most of us never train this area. We need to learn how to have more of a growth mindset, which in short is understanding that obstacles are stepping stones to success. We need to learn to use positive inner voice instead of always criticising ourselves. We need to understand that perfection is not the goal - bettering our self each time we enter the gym is the ultimate goal. The journey is more important than the outcome; therefore, we need to set performance goals rather than outcome goals. We have to learn to praise the athlete for who they are in contrast to what they can do. The only way to train a champion athlete is to train them physically and mentally. This book you have in your hands includes a great chapter on the mental components of cheer.

Finally as an industry leader, I see this book, as well as the full INTENSITY™ Coach Certification enhancing any coach or programme who implements it into their curriculum. The results of training the whole body of the athlete will be forever. They will be strong adults physically and mentally who can deal with the punches life throws in their path. They will be healthier both inwardly and outwardly by learning proper nutritional and workout guidelines.

I wholeheartedly endorse the *Body Before Skill* movement, INTENSITY™ as well as the creators of it. If your passion is to become the best coach, you can be this is a must for your library. I encourage all coaches to take the INTENSITY™ coach qualification. Please join me in my crusade to motivate athletes internally in a positive environment to become better athletes and people of high character and integrity.

2

COACHING CHEERLEADING AS A SPORT

Before we determine if it qualifies as a sport, here is the definition of 'cheerleading' which will be used throughout this book:

Cheerleading represents an activity which promotes athleticism and performance and is characterised by the use of sharp arm movements and enthusiastic expression.

It is also worth noting that this book was not written exclusively for the US cheer community. It addresses cheerleading internationally in various forms and styles, but with one thing in common: we are looking at it as a sport. Some statements throughout this book may or may not resonate with you, but they could hit home with a cheerleader or coach eight time zones away from you - so I ask that you keep an open mind as you read. Hopefully, this book will also bring you a new perspective on certain things, which is never bad thing! Globally, cheerleading exists in different formats which can involve one, some or all the following: vocal cheers, arm motion technique, dance, floor gymnastics, acrobatic stunts, jumps, synchronised choreography and use of pompoms.

Cheerleading can be seen in a number of sub-genres, which include (but are not limited to):

> ‣ **Sideline:** Promotes and supports competing sports teams in a tournament. Can involve stunt and tumbling elements. Poms are often used.

> ‣ **Varsity Cheerleading:** Teams compete against others in an organised tournament usually split by skill level and age.

> ‣ **All-Star Cheerleading:** Private cheerleading training facilities and organisations where the main focus is competitive cheerleading. Poms are not used.

> ‣ **Recreational:** Classes and activities set up for no distinct purposes other than participation, skill attainment and personal development.

> ‣ **Pom Dance:** Main focus is dance skills. Stunts or tumbling skills may be involved but are generally basic and primarily used for visual enhancement. Poms are used throughout or for the majority of the time.

> ‣ **Professional Cheerleading:** Trained dancers performing as a team and supporting a professional sports team (usually receiving a wage for their performance). Stunts and tumbling elements are rarely utilised. Use of poms depends on team and sport (e.g. NFL pro cheerleaders use poms more often than NBA pro cheerleaders do).

Originally, the role of a cheerleading squad was to build team unity and to support athletic teams from the same institution or organisation. While sideline spirit will always remain the core function of school-based cheerleading teams, increased athleticism and participation in competitive events have elevated this activity into the sport we know today.

In 2009, the National Federation of High School Association (NFHS) reported that there were approximately 400,000 participants in high school cheerleading, with around 123,000 on competitive cheer teams.

In 2012 in the USA, only 29 states recognised cheerleading as a sport through their high school athletic associations. The National Collegiate

Athletic Association (NCAA) does not include competitive cheerleading in its roster of sponsored sports. This has a significant impact on the welfare of the athletes since being recognised as a sport can offer certain advantages such as sponsorship, experienced coaching, better equipment, facilities and access to enriched physical preparation. Unfortunately, in many schools athlete welfare is not seriously considered or prioritised.

Outside the world of competitive cheerleading (especially outside the USA), much of the general public only sees the commercial and sideline version of cheer. This is a world totally apart from the sporting side of cheer that we know. It's understandable that the general public is unaware of the competitive side of cheer since most of their opinions are formed from their school experience and what they see on the sidelines of professional sports. The politics of this debate deserves our attention but it does not have a place in this book so will likely pop up on our cheerleading blog on www.cheerobics.net.

In many countries there is no official governing body for cheerleading. In order to create an NGB (national governing body), the country must agree to elect one representative company, among other criteria. In countries with multiple self-determined 'bodies', creating an NGB has proven to be very difficult.

Even though in several countries cheerleading is not a recognised sport per se, it does not mean that competitive cheerleading is any less athletic. Considering that chess is a recognised sport allows us to draw the conclusion that recognition alone does not make it a vigorous activity. The definition of 'sport' is just a word - it doesn't change the nature of the activity. I imagine it would be challenging for anyone who's seen high level competitive cheerleading not to consider it a sport. Those with a low opinion of competitive cheer may have seen it performed at a very amateur level, but just like any other sport it is nonsensical to judge cheerleading based on what it looks like at its lowest level. Take diving for instance. Watching someone belly flop into a pool is not the same as watching Olympic diving, yet they are both called 'diving'.

Another issue with becoming recognised as a sport is the nature of the activity itself. The Women's Sports Foundation recently published a position paper, *Cheerleading, Drill Team, Dancelike and Band as Varsity*

Sports. The most commonly accepted definition of a sport activity includes all the following elements:

> ‣ *A physical activity that involves propelling a mass through space or overcoming the resistance of a mass*
>
> ‣ *A contest or competition against or with an opponent*
>
> ‣ *Is governed by rules that explicitly define the time, space and purpose of the contest and the conditions under which a winner is declared*
>
> ‣ *The acknowledged primary purpose of the competition is a comparison of the relative skills of the participants*

Any physical activity in which relative performance can be judged or quantified can be developed into a competitive sport as long as (1) the physical activity includes the above-defined elements and (2) the primary purpose is competition between teams or individuals within a competitive structure comparable to other sport activities.

Therefore, according to the Women's Sport Foundation, school or sideline cheerleading and similar activities (which are considered support groups for other sports teams) cannot be classified as a sport because they do not fulfil the second requirement, i.e. that its main purpose is competition. It does state, however, that programmes set up for competing purposes (i.e. All-Star cheer or STUNT) should be considered as a sport as they fulfil the second criteria.

If we go by the definition of 'sport' in the Oxford Dictionary as "an activity involving physical exertion and skill in which an individual or team competes against another or others for entertainment", then whether cheerleading is competitive or sideline, officially recognised or not, there is no doubt that cheerleading is a sport.

As you can see, defining cheerleading as an official sport is a very complex matter. Rather than being a question of right or wrong, it is a question of what we want our industry to look like. Of course, being recognised officially would bring much more funding, support, safety and regulations, but we would need to accept that much of the freedom we currently have to shape our industry would no longer exist.

Regardless of the label, within the industry we should recognise cheer as a sport and train our cheerleaders accordingly. Everything we do should be to the benefit the development of our athletes to ensure that safety, training and management guidelines emulate those of other international sports.

Despite public perception, an increasing number of countries worldwide are recognising cheerleading as a sport and are becoming involved in international championships. As these numbers grow, and with more and more countries focusing on overall public health and particular inclusion of females in sport, we expect the popularity, funding and recognition of cheerleading to grow exponentially over the next decade.

> *What if cheerleading becomes an Olympic sport?*
> *What if it never does?*
> *Should this change the way we train our athletes?*

Regardless of the answer, the mission of *Body Before Skill* is simple: to set a strong foundation for building more resilient, trainable and high-achieving athletes. Cheerleading is a sport, so let's build better athletes.

DANGERS & INJURY

In October 2012, the American Academy of Pediatrics released a set of new guidelines and a policy statement to help prevent cheerleading injuries. According to the AAP, cheerleading has accounted for approximately 66% of all catastrophic injuries in high school athletes over the past 25 years.

Cheerleading injuries in the US accounted for 4954 hospital emergency visits in 1980. This number increased by over 400% to 26 786 hospital visits in 2007.

Using a calculation of 'athletic exposure' (1 unit = 1 athlete participating in 1 practice or competition), cheerleading rated a 0.9 on average on 1000 exposures for overall injury and a range of 0.5 to an exceptionally high 1.62 on catastrophic injury, which places it at the top of the injury league. Separated by institutions, we see that the rates are:

college (2.4), elementary school (1.5), high school (0.9) all-star (0.8), middle school (0.5) and recreational cheerleaders (0.5).

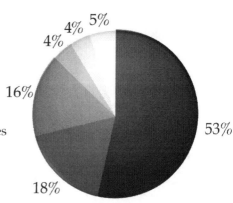

- Sprains & strains
- Abrasions & contusions
- Fractures & dislocations
- Lacerations & punctures
- Concussions & head injuries
- Other

Though these stats are alarming, there is significant data to show that cheerleading has experienced vast improvements in injury rates over the past ten years since safety guidelines were implemented by the American Association of Cheerleading Coaches and Administrators (AACCA), National Cheer Safety Foundation (NCSF) and the United States All Star Federation (USASF). These regulations were put into place after 12 high school and college catastrophic injuries occurred in 2005-2006. Just five years later, the *National Centre for Catastrophic Sport Injury Research* published data showing that by 2010 there were 358 direct catastrophic injuries for football compared with only 62 for cheer and that the percentage of collegiate injuries was reduced by almost half. The AAP lists a number of risk factors linked to cheerleading injuries:

- Higher BMI
- Previous injury
- Cheering on hard surfaces
- Performing stunts above critical height
- Supervision by a coach with a low level of training experience

Data collected in the past decade also shows that the highest percentage of injuries in cheerleading are sprains and strains. While these are comparatively low-level injuries, they should be the exception to regular cheerleading training - not the rule. Sprains and strains are induced by excessive force onto the joint, causing it to move beyond its range of motion. They are likely due to poor control over a movement performing skills when ill-prepared (i.e. not warming up and stretching enough before exercises or stretching too much before power training) and weak joints due to insufficient strength and conditioning. This is why it is extremely important that coaches and athletes understand how to adequately prepare joints for exercise and ensure that training conditions are adequate for the demands of the activity.

Since the newest safety regulations were introduced in 2007, it is encouraging to see that the relative number of injuries (injury rate versus participation), and more importantly, the number of catastrophic injuries are decreasing significantly. As a community, we are on the right track for making cheerleading a safer activity for all participants.

There is evidence to show that many cheerleaders and teams have never experienced drastic levels of injury. However, in many cases, the lack of recognition as a sport prevents many athletes and coaches from gaining access to necessary training, information and purpose-built equipment, all factors which increase the risk of injury.

Those programmes with a firm grasp and dedicated implementation of the suggested safety guidelines combined with a good understanding of the physicality of cheerleading, demonstrate that cheerleading can be a perfectly safe activity. Many programmes have shown little or significantly less injury incidents than the quoted data despite their high level of performance.

Given that coach education so clearly affects athlete safety, it is up to industry professionals and organisations to strive for the best information they can access for the welfare of their teams. This includes a solid understanding of the safety guidelines set by the USASF, NCAA, and NFHS. The Journal of American Academy of Pediatrics also offered some useful insight, in a report suggesting the following as the five principles of injury prevention:

- Cheerleaders should have a pre-participation physical examination before participating in a cheerleading programme and should have access to appropriate strength and conditioning programmes.

- Cheerleaders should be supervised by qualified coaches who have been trained and certified in proper spotting for gymnastic elements and partner stunts, safety measures and basic injury management.

- Cheerleaders should be trained in proper spotting techniques and should only attempt stunts after they have demonstrated appropriate skill progression and proficiency required to complete the stunt. Spotters and bases should have sufficient upper body and core strength and balance to support flyers.

- Cheerleaders should follow a nutrition plan that is suitable to their training demands

- Coaches need to take responsibility for the welfare of their athletes by increasing the amount of conditioning incorporated in training to prevent injury and enabling their athletes' bodies to be adequately prepared for the physical demands of the skills.

Throughout this book we will explore how particular aspects of training can not only enhance athletic ability but also reduce the risk of injury when learning new skills training for competitions and throughout all parts of the cheerleading season. So sit back, open your mind and have highlighters, pens and post-its ready. We have left plenty of spaces in this book that you can use to make notes, jot down ideas, doodle, scribble or anything that is going to help you get the most out of what we have put together for you.

SKILL DEVELOPMENT

One of the downsides of cheerleading not being a recognised sport is that there are few strict guidelines (in contrast to gymnastics, for example) on how athletes should progress to the next level. The concept of following the right 'progression' is used a lot within our industry, but there are no industry standards as to how long an athlete has to spend preparing for a certain skill before attempting another one. There is constant pressure to make sure an athlete 'gets his roundoff-backhandspring-backtuck for Nationals' for example, even if this is a rushed and unrealistic goal.

The mantra of 'following progressions' is one of the most abused within cheerleading. We are aware of them but the guidelines are so blurred that there is much more room for gambling 'skill vs execution' at competitions than in a gymnastics meet. A number of event producers are moving towards a scoring system that addresses this, but it is by no means widespread (at the time of writing). It is therefore the responsibility of coaches to lead by example to focus on long-term athlete development and safety.

Within cheerleading, placing the athlete at a particular level is usually dependent on:

> ‣ Team placement at tryouts (athletes with set skills are placed within teams according to execution levels versus spots on the team)
>
> ‣ Coaches strategically deciding which division to enter athletes based on on which other teams are competing, the score sheet and overall perceived ability of the team
>
> ‣ Goals set by the coaches for the season

Hopefully, as an industry we can develop a more conscientious understanding the physical and welfare requirements of keeping athletes to the right level, and making sure that they are fully maximising their potential at that level before moving on. The first step is to understand how athletes learn a new skill and how different athletes vary.

SKILL ACQUISITION

Let's think about what happens when an athlete learns a new perceptual motor skills. The action involves thought, interpretation and movement. There are several schools of thought in respect to learning theory of perceptual motor skills, and the *Fitts & Posner* (1967) model is the one most commonly used within the sports industry. This describes three stages of learning:

- **Cognitive phase:** Identification and development of the component parts of the skill – involves formation of a mental picture of the skill.

- **Associative phase:** Linking the component parts into a smooth action – involves practicing the skill and using feedback to perfect the skill.

- **Autonomous phase:** Developing the learned skill so that it becomes automatic – involves little or no conscious thought or attention whilst performing the skill. Not all athletes reach this stage.

It is essential that coaches communicate information effectively during the cognitive phase and then guide this understanding to the associative stage. That way, the athlete will be mostly responsible for the mastery of the skill during the autonomous phase.

The three methods of learning are visual, verbal (auditory) or active (kinaesthetic). Within sports we can identify eight learning profiles, each requiring different coaching and correction methods. Most athletes will exhibit a combination of a number of learning profiles:

- **Active:** These athletes prefer learning through active participation, like performing a stunt or tumbling drill. They usually prefer to work in groups. These learners can act without thinking and can often skip progressions. It is best to help them perform the skill with minimal instruction and to provide feedback in the form of FEEL (e.g. "imagine a string pulling you up from the top of your head").

‣ **Reflective:** These athletes prefer to think about an exact skill/strategy before executing it. Put time aside for athletes to review or question specific skills or instructions. Be aware that athletes who overthink things can be more reluctant to try new skills and have a tendency towards mental blocks. Visualisation, using verbal queues and allocating some 'thinking time' before the skill will be beneficial for this type of athlete.

‣ **Sensing:** These athletes prefer to follow previously tested techniques when learning new skills. They like learning technical information about the skill and how it is built. They can be reluctant to unknown approaches or surprises. Demonstration of any new technique or skill will be essential.

‣ **Intuitive:** These athletes are more open to innovative approaches and techniques. They can be helpful when the coach is experimenting with a new element of new choreography but should refine the skill before teaching their 'sensing' teammates. Repetition with these athletes can lead to boredom, so it can be more productive for them to have varied activities within one session.

‣ **Visual:** These athletes need to see a skill being demonstrated before they can consciously transform it into action. It is essential that coaches give a full, technically sound demonstration of the skill to be achieved. If impossible with athletes in-house, coaches can use media if this provides a better example. It is equally important to remove the demonstration of bad techniques (i.e. "don't do THIS") because athletes will still retain the visual information, regardless if it is incorrect.

‣ **Verbal:** These athletes prefer spoken instruction on how to perform the skill. Even though this is the easiest and most common type of coaching, it is statistically the least preferred learning style by athletes. Whenever using this method, pair it with some form of positive visual instruction to ensure words are explained through images (since a picture is worth a thousand words).

‣ **Sequential:** These athletes gather and understand information in logical steps ensuring each element is tested individually before piecing everything together. "Progressions," drills and determining exactly what needs to be done on each count is key to this type of learning profile.

‣ **Global:** These athletes like to understand the overall picture before filling in the details. They often struggle or become frustrated when asked to execute only a small part of the element without having seen its place within the sequence. Helping them understand the value of narrow focus when learning something new and a firm but patient approach with any resulting challenging behaviour is key to this athlete's learning style.

Understanding the learning profiles of your athletes will enable the cognitive and associative phase of learning to be faster and more effective. Even though it may be impossible to cater to everyone, including all elements within your coaching style will enable your team to understand directions more easily and will make sure your training time more efficient (guaranteeing you less time spent banging your head against the gym wall).

PERFECTING SKILLS

Several theories have been presented in respect to the mastery of skill. You may have come across Malcolm Gladwell's *Outliers* which explores the theory put forward by Simon & Chase (1973) that it takes 10,000 hours of deliberate practice before a skill is mastered. It is important, however, to understand that even though the amount of practice time is a crucial element, it is not the sole contributor to success. Imagine an athlete has never learned the correct technique for a specific skill. They could drill the skill as they know it for 10,000 hours and at the end of this time, they would have only mastered something useless or potentially dangerous. 10,000 hours spent embedding incorrect techniques in an athlete's muscle memory is an absolute waste of learning time because it takes much longer to un-learn it than to start the skill from scratch.

Time is a relative measure when it comes to skill acquisition. To understand how long it should take each individual athlete to fully master a particular skill will depend on:

> ‣ **Body awareness:** An athlete's understanding of their own muscles, joints, skeletal structure, breathing, speed, flexibility, relative position to others/the floor/the air, etc. and how skill elements affect their body.

> ‣ **Body composition:** What makes up their body, including fat percentage, lean muscle mass, ratio of fast-twitch and slow-twitch, bone density, VO2max, etc.

> ‣ **Natural ability:** Also known as *'kinaesthetic intelligence'*, the natural rate at which an athlete can use their body to perform the skill with minimal time spent in the cognitive phase.

> ‣ **Genetics:** The athlete's innate ability to react, be flexible, be strong, be fast, utilise oxygen, endure, sustain possible injury and any other physical factor without training.

> ‣ **Physical trainability:** The margin between the athlete's 'bottom line' and their 'top line' (maximum potential) of genetic capability through athletic training.

> ‣ **Confidence:** The athlete's belief in their own skill and potential, leading to strong, deliberate visualisation and mental resilience.

> ‣ **Cognitive ability:** The athlete's ability to receive and process new instruction.

> ‣ **Approach to feedback:** The athlete's willingness to take feedback and effect a physical change in their action.

All of these factors play a part in the athlete's transition from the cognitive and associative phases to the autonomous phase of perfecting the skill (i.e. being able to execute the skill with the correct technique repeatedly). It is only once the athlete has arrived at this stage that a skill will be embedded as muscle memory. What is important to understand in the term 'muscle memory' is that it's not a memory stored in the muscles (such as an involuntary contraction like a heart beat) but rather a **procedural memory** stored within the brain. This is our long-term memory, responsible for letting us know how to perform certain actions without thinking about them while doing them, like tying your shoelaces or walking.

Building procedural memory happens as we repeat a certain sequence over and over again. It is important to note that when building procedural memory, the body does not differentiate between an action or skill performed correctly or incorrectly. As such, it is crucial that the skill is consistently drilled with the right technique during the initial two learning phases. This is also why it's detrimental or even dangerous to perform a skill with improper technique when the muscles are fatigued.

Procedural memory is extremely difficult to reverse (think of how hard it is to learn a different way to tie your shoelaces!) so you can save your time and that of your athletes by ensuring skill technique is perfected before drilling a high number of repetitions.

MAXIMISING SKILLS: 7 TO 10

Maximising skill means achieving the maximum score available for the execution of that skill. At times, athletes might be able to perform the skill safely whilst lacking technical finesse and mastery. I coined the '7-to-10 concept' as a way to describe what transforms a good skill into a great skill and therefore, a good team into a great team. Whereas an athlete could happily score a 7 out of 10 with an autonomous skill, there is still a 30% range of improvement possible. The 7-to-10 concept is based on:

- ‣ Understanding that achieving a skill is not the final goal. The end goal should be achieving the skill flawlessly.
- ‣ Understanding that achieving the skill is not a sign that the athlete is ready for the next progression. The skill needs to be technically sound and consistent before moving on.
- ‣ Understanding *what it feels like* to perform the skill at '10' as opposed to '7'.

- ‣ The athlete being able to perform the skill consistently in 'full out' conditions or during long training sessions without execution being compromised.
- ‣ The athlete being fully confident in their own ability to perform the skill.
- ‣ The body being at its physical optimum to perform the skill to the best of its ability.
- ‣ The athlete eating and drinking appropriately for the work required.
- ‣ The body being given sufficient time to recover.

One trick I tend to use a lot with athletes is giving them quantifiable feedback. Instead of asking them to perform better, jump higher, tumble faster, I like to give them a number. For example: *"I know you are able to perform at an 8 but right now you're giving me 6. Tell me what you need to do to get an 8 and then show it to me"*. I am very careful to avoid using 9s or 10s with individual athletes so that they always have something to strive for. This also avoids encouraging a fixed mindset (a trick I learned from teachers in the Italian schooling system, where the scale was 1-10 but the scores were never given below 4 or above 8 for this precise purpose). If asked *"when will I get a 10?,"* I usually get away with saying that the day I award a 10 would be a very sad one as I would have to ship them off to the olympic trials because I have nothing left to teach them.

3

BUILDING COMPLETE ATHLETES

In the fitness industry, the term *total fitness* is used to describe a person who achieves complete balance in all elements of their existence. This includes physical, nutritional, mental, environmental, psychological, spiritual, behavioural and social. Similarly, the *360 Athlete* concept symbolises the person who achieves the overall combination of the fitness elements required to fulfil the demands of the *Body Before Skill* concept. Missing or underdeveloped components of total fitness can result in both a limit to the performance of some skills and the potential for preventable injuries. The main factors that limit an athlete in this area are:

- ‣ Poor body awareness
- ‣ The neglect of certain fitness elements
- ‣ Exertion of the body beyond what it is capable of

These problem areas are most commonly found in athletes who train less frequently, do not have an athletic background, or who work with coaches who do not understand the value and importance of total fitness. It is more common to find these factors in children/teens whose parents did not have a sporting or athletic childhood. While cheerleading involves many intricate and specific skills, achieving a basic level of fitness and correcting initial bad habits can help to overcome most of the challenges and performance plateaus at levels 1 through to 6.

Throughout the rest of the book we'll explore the most common limiting factors and how they affect performance. We'll also provide advice and solutions to see improvement. The 7 elements that make up the total fitness of an athlete are:

‣ **Strength and Endurance:** How much force can the athlete physically exert and for how long?

‣ **Speed and Power:** How quickly can the athlete move and with what degree of explosive force?

‣ **Stability:** How controlled is the body in performing skills and how does this translate into execution, consistency and injury prevention?

‣ **Cardiovascular Fitness:** How effectively can the body process and utilise oxygen?

‣ **Flexibility:** What is the athlete's range of movement?

‣ **Motor Skills:** Can the athlete control their movement? Do their bodies work as they want them to?

‣ **Nutrition:** Are they eating and drinking the right foods to fuel their athletic activity?

‣ **Mindset:** Do athletes have the correct mindset to learn and perform new skills? Do they believe they are capable of learning and performing well?

STRENGTH & ENDURANCE

Muscular strength and endurance are the first elements that come to mind when we think of athlete fitness since most activities require both strength and endurance to varying degrees. Endurance is the body's ability to sustain exercise over a period of time. It relates to the efficiency of the muscles, the efficiency with which an athlete uses oxygen and fuel, the stability of the joints, and the consistency of the exercise. The difference between strength and endurance is:

> ‣ **Muscular strength:** the maximum amount of force that a muscle can exert against some form of resistance in a single effort

> ‣ **Muscular endurance:** the ability of a muscle or muscle group to work continuously / for a long time without tiring

Muscular strength and endurance training will improve sports and everyday performance, as well as improve the body's shape and tone (which ultimately contributes to self-esteem and confidence). The process of the muscles becoming stronger is known as **hypertrophy,** an increase in muscle fibre size. This is most commonly achieved through training and proper nutrition (by including more protein in the diet, for example).

There are two methods of training hypertrophy:

> ‣ **Sarcoplasmic** (visual) Increasing the volume of fluid in the muscle cell - growth is visual rather than functional, or

> ‣ **Myofibrillar** (functional) Increasing the proteins in the muscle - growth is functional rather than visual. This is the one that is useful for sports performance.

To train functional muscle athletes need to:

> ‣ **Train to failure** (i.e. until your body can take no more, this is individual to each athlete) or leave one final rep if using weights, for safety.
>
> ‣ **Take short rest periods**, 30–90 seconds. Rest-pause techniques can also be effective.
>
> ‣ **Prioritise muscle efficiency** instead of adding more muscle / building strength.
>
> ‣ **Perform 12–20 sets per muscle group** (e.g. this could include 4 sets each of squats, lunges, box jumps and side lunges to equal 16 sets focusing on the glutes, hamstrings and quadriceps). Supersets can help to add volume and improve efficiency.
>
> ‣ **Consume a minimum 1g of protein** per pound of bodyweight (2g per kg).

Specific Adaptation to Imposed Demand (SAID Principle) teaches us that the body gets used to the training it is given. Essentially, if you squat a lot, you will become good at squats. Variety, as well as *progressive overload* (i.e. adding reps, resistance or changing training conditions) is therefore key to achieving overall strength development in an athlete.

The shape and strength of the muscle will depend on the type of movement executed. It is therefore possible for athletes to be very strong but not to have a bulky appearance (in females more so than males). For example, a professional ballet dancer is shaped very differently from a professional field athlete (javelin, shot put, discus etc), but both have a great deal of muscular strength and endurance.

Calisthenic exercises (using one's own body weight as resistance) can be very effective ways of training strength and endurance when gym equipment/weights are not available. Athletes across the world can train their conditioning regardless of the equipment they have access to. I believe all athletes should have the same opportunities to develop their bodies which is why the INTENSITY™ method focuses on calisthenics. Furthermore, if you can lift a light weight slowly, you can lift a heavy weight quickly. Athletes can do strength training with lighter weights (in this case, their own body weight) but still enjoy the benefits of improving their top-line absolute strength.

> ‣ **To improve strength:** Perform exercises using more body weight, holding the contraction for a shorter time and with fewer repetitions, (e.g. 123 push-ups, victory hollowman/ superman) - typically 8-16 reps max per set.
>
> ‣ **To improve endurance:** Perform exercises using less body weight for longer periods of time and by increasing repetitions, (e.g. crunches, tricep dips, standard push-ups) - 16-32 reps or even higher, depending on the specific exercise.

We also need to remember that strength and endurance are relative to the individual athlete. For training to be effective, we shouldn't ask or expect all members of the gym to follow the exact same training regimen to gain the same degree of results. Just like tumbling progressions, conditioning progressions have to be followed as well, especially when dealing with athletes of varying degrees of fitness within a single team. Just as you would not teach level 5 tumbling skills to level 1 athletes, relevant training must also consider the strength and endurance of those being trained.

Relevant training is significant in all aspects of total fitness but especially relevant to strength and endurance because technical execution at the right weight is far more beneficial than poor execution at a level that is too advanced. For example, an athlete who struggles to complete five full body push-ups needs the option of performing a full set from the knees with correct technique.

It has become popular with certain teams to practice 'extreme conditioning' such as sets of back-handspring-burpees or burpee-back-tucks. Yes, don't they look so wonderfully impressive on social media? The trouble with these drills is that, unless they are performed by highly skilled athletes with a high level of fitness and very good technical execution, they can be extremely dangerous. They can even be counter-productive, not only to strength and endurance training but also to their muscle memory. When training for strength and endurance, there are a number of variables you can manipulate to create the right degree of challenge for the athlete. The variables to consider are:

‣ **Motor skill:** Is the athlete able to complete the skill autonomously and is it technically correct? *Example:* Can the athlete hold the plank position correctly and adjust the resistance where needed? *Adaptation:* Their skill execution must be solid and consistent throughout every repetition before the plank should be used as a conditioning drill.

‣ **Load:** The weight of the body created by the distance between the lever and the pivot. *Example:* The weight of the athlete when doing pushups on their toes as opposed as from the knees. *Adaptation:* Adjust the load by decreasing the distance between the base of support (arms) and the fulcrum (point against where the lever turns or is supported). Therefore to make the pushup easier you would holdup on the knees instead of from the feet.

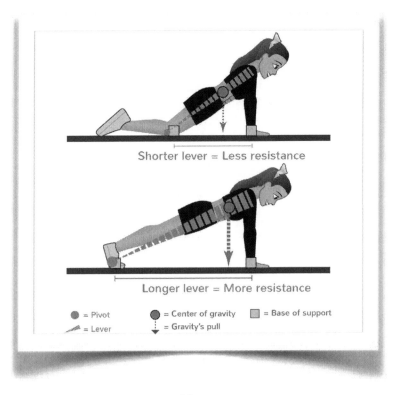

Shorter lever = Less resistance

Longer lever = More resistance

● = Pivot   ● = Center of gravity   ▢ = Base of support
⬎ = Lever   ⋮ = Gravity's pull

‣ **Resistance:** The total amount of weight that the body has to work against. *Example:* The athlete's weight, the mechanical advantage and the strength of the muscles. *Adaptation:* Reduce or increase the load to adjust the resistance required.

‣ **Speed of execution:** How fast are the athletes performing each repetition? *Example:* Performing push-ups to music speed with a 140bpm track. *Adaptation:* Decrease or increase the music speed or use double or half counts (such as completing the movement with 1-2-3-4 speed instead of 1-2).

‣ **Energy availability:** How much energy does the athlete have available at this specific time? *Example:* Athletes doing a series of pushups after completing a fullout routine instead of doing it after warmup. Or doing pushups one hour vs. five hours after having a snack. *Adaptation:* Drill conditioning at different times during practices so that strength and endurance are trained at different stages of fatigue.

‣ **Training conditions:** How are the external factors (such as temperature and humidity) affecting the athletes' effort? *Example:* Doing push-ups on a hard floor during the summer in high humidity. *Adaptation:* Consider how the training conditions can be affecting your athletes and adapt your training plan accordingly.

‣ **Repetitions (**reps): How many repetitions of each exercise is being repeated within one set? *Example:* 12 full push-ups being completed in a set. *Adaptation:* Increase the number of reps the athlete can perform easily by adding a number of reps to achieve more effort or maximum exertion.

‣ **Sets:** How many sets of exercises are being performed? *Example:* 3 sets of 12 reps. *Adaptation:* Set a minimum of 2 sets and increase to 3 or 4 depending on the time available and the athlete's conditioning level.

‣ **Rest period:** How many seconds of rest is the athlete taking between each set or different exercises? *Example:* 30 seconds rest in between push-up sets. *Adaptation:* Try to keep rest periods between sets and repetitions at 15-30 seconds, only allowing 1-2min when training at above 80% heart rate.

It is important to know that true strength does not work in isolation (i.e. having strong arms or legs). Instead, it is every kinetic chain of the body working together and activating maximum strength for a particular movement. A typical example is basing a stunt: Some bases focus on their arm strength to lift. Experienced bases know that it's their legs which gives them lift power. Unfortunately, the vast majority of bases forget that their core is responsible for supporting the movement of the rest of their body. In cheerleading, having a weak core is equivalent to a large tree with heavy branches and strong roots but a thin trunk. Against wind, that tree will bend or snap. Equally, poor use of the legs will make all arm effort pointless as the lift momentum has to be created by the larger of the two muscle groups (i.e. legs, not arms).

This is precisely how the INTENSITY™ programme was developed as opposed to any other fitness programme currently available. It is designed to build strength and endurance through *skill specificity* and by linking all the muscles together in movement.

SPEED & POWER

Power is the combination of strength with speed. It is one aspect of fitness that is especially relevant to cheerleading but is frequently overlooked as a training concept. Let's use the toe touch as an example. It is common knowledge that a good toe touch requires strong hip flexors, strong adductors, a strong core and good flexibility. A cheerleader who has all of these may still struggle to perform a great toe touch because their fast-twitch muscle fibres are weaker than their slow-twitch muscle fibres. In other words, they struggle to channel their power at speed. They find it difficult to complete the full movement within a certain timeframe, so the jump will be either slow or low. Training athletes in speed and power will enable them to perform their full range of motion and strength in a shorter amount of time. This will increase their speed and, therefore, the level of execution. Power comes as a consequence of:

- **Selective recruitment:** Fast-twitch muscle fibres cannot be created but they can be trained to become larger, stronger and faster by repeating short, fast bursts of exercises. Longer repetitions target the durability of slow-twitch muscles.

- **Targeted muscle sequencing:** Individual skill elements require plyometric training, such as the snap of the leg in a toe touch. Instead of drilling the full toe-touch repeatedly (which would create unnecessary fatigue), you can using drill exercises like kick drills to train the snap of the leg on each side of the body in rapid sequence.

The ability to perform certain skills with ease, power and speed depends on a number of factors. Effective drills are designed to develop selective recruitment of the fast-twitch fibres through targeted muscle sequencing without requiring additional equipment. Train using:

- **Plyometric training:** Stretching and contracting a muscle in rapid sequence until failure (e.g. frog jumps)

- **Explosive strength training:** Low number of repetitions (2 or 3 maximum) at the highest maximum force the body can sustain, using explosive power (e.g. 3 jumps to best ability)

When training speed and power, we need to take into consideration:

> ‣ **Range of motion:** The movement required and how far the athlete can perform this safely without causing injury (e.g. maximum range on toe touch position).

> ‣ **Relative strength:** The relationship between the maximum body strength and the mass, to reduce the time it takes to perform the range of motion (e.g. length and weight of the leg compared to the strength of the muscles required for the lift).

> ‣ **Inertia and keeping momentum:** Newton's 1st Law of Motion (every object in a state of uniform motion tends to remain in that state of motion unless an external force is applied to it). Athletes need to pay attention to keep momentum going between moves to avoid additional effort (e.g. absorbing and springing back up in-between jumps instead of landing 'dead').

> ‣ **An action requires an opposite reaction:** Newton's 3rd Law of Motion, (for every action, there is an equal and opposite reaction). The athlete needs to apply an equal amount of force against the ground to create an upwards force (e.g. bending and then pushing hard to jump up).

> ‣ **Reactivity:** The responsiveness of the neuromuscular system, (e.g. the fastest music BPM that the body can keep up with when doing kick drills or the jump itself to its full range).

> ‣ **Technical ability:** How well the athlete can perform the skill and hold the full body position if the element of effort is removed (e.g. performing the toe touch on a trampoline).

> ‣ **Progressive overload:** How much additional physical stress the athlete can sustain when performing the muscle sequence with additional weight or elements (e.g. completing the full toe touch instead of just the jump kick drill).

CARDIOVASCULAR FITNESS

Cardiovascular (CV) fitness is the term used to assess the efficiency of the lungs, heart and circulatory system in transporting and utilising oxygen throughout the body. In cheerleading, having good CV fitness is extremely important so that athletes can correctly perform skills at any point in a full out routine as well as through extensive training sessions of over 90 minutes. We often see athletes perform a skill correctly over and over again in isolation or even within a sequence, yet they find it difficult to hit the skill in the context of a full routine. Often, this is due to the athlete's CV endurance threshold not being on par with the total energy and endurance required to perform all the skills in combination. Muscles without enough oxygen are unable to sustain the skill within a full out routine which can be very frustrating. Frustrated coaches often misdiagnose the cause of the skill that won't hit, asking the athletes to repeat the sequence over and over again which only tires them out more.

The problem is that by this point, the issue of endurance cannot be fixed. The body needs a minimum of 2-3 months to increase its level of endurance so that all skills can be consistent. Cheerleaders need to train their endurance as well as individual skills; or all their efforts may go to waste when it comes to putting the skills together in a full routine. We should train using **aerobic and anaerobic exercise** in order to fully maximise the way athletes' bodies copes with repetition training.

Having better cardiovascular fitness indicates a stronger heart that pumps a higher volume of blood per stroke, an expanded capillary network and increased number of mitochondria in cells. This means that the body transports oxygen more efficiently and becomes more adaptive to aerobic activity. There are two important elements that indicate an athlete's cardiovascular fitness:

- **Heart rate:** The lower the heart rate is during the full out routine, the easier it will be for athletes to execute the skills.

- **VO2 max:** The total volume of oxygen that the athlete's body is able to make use of during exercise. This includes the volume that the lungs are able to take in as well as a good network of capillaries to distribute the oxygen to the muscles so that they can keep working past the anaerobic threshold.

% MHR	Estimated HR	Purpose
30 - 40%	70 - 80	Rest
50 – 60%	100 - 120	Improve CV Fitness for untrained individuals
60 - 70%	120 - 135	Fat Burn (aerobic)
70 - 80%	135 - 155	Base of CV Fitness (aerobic + anaerobic)
80 - 90%	155 - 170	Improving CV fitness for athletes (aerobic + anaerobic)
90 – 100%	170+	Anaerobic performance zone

An athlete can significantly improve their performance on the mat by developing these two variables, as long as these are included in their training from the beginning of the season.

When we think of stamina and endurance for cheerleading, the first thing that springs to mind is what's required in order to perform skills over the length of a 2:30min cheer routine. However, the majority of our industry fails to consider the concept of training for the competition weekend as a whole. Even if athletes are well-trained to endure a 2:30min full out routine, they are not always trained to withstand the physical demands of a competition weekend.

Let me compare a full weekend of competition to when I was filming for the INTENSITY™ DVD series. The full series is made up of 8 individual workouts of 20min each where the heart rate works anywhere from 50% of MHR (on the Flex DVD) to upwards of 60-90% on some of the other workouts. Each workout needed to be filmed about three or four time along with tutorial videos. I knew the shoot would be held over four days with ten hours of filming scheduled for each day. To prepare, in the months preceding the shoot I made sure I was not just training for the execution of each individual workout: I had to build up my resistance and endurance for an exhausting forty hours. Thankfully I managed to get through it with just one minor leg cramp (which of course, was also caught on camera!).

When we train our athletes for a competition, we are usually just preparing them for the 2:30min on the mat. We increase the number of full outs and add more hours of practice. It's almost like we are training our athletes for a 1000m run, but we're also expecting them to run a marathon the day before. It's no surprise that the amount of injuries increase in proximity of competitions. This is why solid cardiovascular training is necessary in cheerleading so that athletes can tackle different types of endurance demands. We need to train our athletes for:

> ‣ **Full outs:** Performance of a full cheer routine including all skill elements with heart rate going between 70% - 90% for 2.5 minutes, using alactic respiration (short-term anaerobic respiration that lasts up to the first 90seconds of exercises) mixed with aerobic respiration (utilising oxygen). Depending on the athlete and their body's ability to use the different energy systems (and their level of fatigue at the time of execution) the ratio of cheer routines generally use 70% anaerobic respiration to 30% aerobic.

> ‣ **Intensive weekends:** Long training sessions or competition weekends where training can extend over two or three hours multiple times over a few days. The heart rate will fluctuate from rest to 90% at different times throughout the day, causing the trigger of three energy systems.

Cardiovascular fitness can also be a very useful way of reducing overall body fat percentage if some athletes want to achieve a leaner physique. Cardiovascular activity increases our metabolic rate and, when training in the 60-80% zone, the heart rate is optimal for burning calories (as long as exercise is performed for a minimum of 20 minutes and the athlete has not consumed carbohydrates within 2 hours of training). The formula to estimate someone's estimated maximum heart rate is:

MAXIMUM HEART RATE (mHR)   =   220 - AGE

For example, if you wanted to calculate the estimated maximum heart rate for a 25 year old, subtract 25 from 220, to give you 195. This represents the 100% heart rate and based on this number, you can then calculate the appropriate training zone percentage. To be 100% accurate, athletes can have their mHR tested at a medical clinic or sports performance centre.

To calculate the heart rate during rest/exercise, you can find the pulse (on the thumb-side of wrist, below the palm) and count the number of beats for 15 seconds then multiply by 4 (or just calculate the total beats in one minute).

There are 3 approaches to cardiovascular fitness:

> ‣ **Continuous:** Requires a minimum of 20 minutes of aerobic exercise. This is difficult to monitor unless you're in a fitness or dance class, or exercising at a steady regulated pace such as jogging.
> ‣ **Fartlek:** Varying the pace and speed of movements over a more extended period of time. A regular cheerleading practice is an example of this.
> ‣ **Interval:** Timed and alternating short bursts of high intensity exercises with low intensity exercises.

The most effective way of increasing the heart rate is to utilise the larger muscle groups of the body: gluteus maximus, hamstrings and quadriceps. This is because they require our bodyweight to work against resistance, creating a greater effort. Movements that require jumping, bending and travelling are more effective. These types of movements should be mixed to create a balance of high intensity and low intensity to avoid repetitive strain injury and stress to the joints and muscles.

The upper body uses smaller muscles, so moving them on their own is not an effective way to raise the heart rate. Moving the arms above the head is going to elevate the heart rate because blood is rushing down the arms against the force of gravity. Even though this helps to increase the heart rate, it is not as a consequence of oxygen deficiency so it is of little value in terms of cardiovascular fitness. When using arm exercises, include moves above the shoulder level (touchdowns and High Vs) at no more than 30% of the duration of the routine and alternate them with a few counts of low arm motions.

To improve cardiovascular fitness, athletes must:

> ‣ **Train cardiovascular exercise 2-3 times a week** between 60-80% heart rate for 20-60min of continuous exercise outside of training. **Bring the heart rate to over 80%** for 3 x 5 minutes at least three times a week (such as fast sprints or INTENSITY™ workouts).
>
> ‣ **Use larger muscle groups.**
>
> ‣ **Train at an appropriate heart rate,** progressively increasing the intensity and endurance.
>
> ‣ **Train skills with progressive overload** techniques and at different heart rates.

STABILITY

Stability describes our body's ability to stay centred and in full control when an external force such as gravity, impact, motion, or resistance is applied. When we refer to stability, we're referring to the body as a whole and the individual systems and joints within the body. Joint stability is determined by a number factors:

 ▸ **Balance:** Our ability to stay upright is controlled by the inner ears, our eyes and our body awareness.

 ▸ **Centre of gravity:** This is usually located within our bodies at about a third of our height. It is the point that stabilises us with gravity depending on our weight, height and shape. The centre of gravity will be different when we are in an inverted position. Furthermore, the closer the centre of gravity is to the ground, the more stable we are, so shorter people are naturally more stable because of a lower centre of gravity.

 ▸ **Posture and alignment:** Maintaining good posture and correct alignment of the joints will have a huge impact upon the stability of the athlete. Not only it will prevent some form of injuries caused by impact on improper alignment, it will also allow the muscles and momentum to work together to give the right trajectory to the movement, making the skill far easier than it would be with an incorrect posture.

 ▸ **Core:** The muscles that we refer to as the 'core' are the transversus abdominis (TVA), pelvic floor, obliques, multifidus and psoas. These are stabiliser muscles that are found under the rectus abdominis (abs) and are therefore not fully visible. These muscles are key to strength and stability in sports but are the most neglected because they cannot be seen. Training and strengthening these muscles in isolation will hugely impact the athlete's ability to be in full control of their skills and coordinate all required body mechanics.

 ▸ **Joint strength:** Joints are weakened with stretching. When the tendons and ligaments are continually pushed beyond their limits, their elasticity is reduced and they are less able to support the joints. With continuous impact, joints will weaken and be more likely to suffer an injury. Consequently, sprains and strains are major issues within cheerleading. They are not necessarily due to lack of stretching; on the contrary, they are mainly due to excessive stretching without any strengthening counter-work.

Stability can't be trained in the same way as strength or power. Speed, resistance and repetitions are not useful in this case. Instead, some ways to challenge and train stability include:

- **Inversions:** Performing handstands, headstands, etc. These will target core muscles, centre of gravity, posture and upper body joints which require the most strengthening. Upper body joints are used less frequently, but when we put them to work with cheer skills they take a high proportion of body weight in comparison to the lower body.

- **Dynamic stability exercises:** Moving from one position into another, repeatedly, keeping rhythm and form. Concentrating on keeping movements clean and inexpensive in energy. To challenge this further, stand on a wobble board or stability ball. This will target the core, overall balance, ankle and knee joint stability.

- **Progressive overload:** Performing exercises by gradually overloading resistance force against the stability. For example training a shape on the ground versus training it on higher ground or an unstable surface, or holding a weight. Anything that would push the body to fight harder to stay stable.

- **Under physical stress:** Performing stability exercises when the muscles are fatigued and the heart rate is above 70%. Practicing a stunt on a stunt-stand when athletes are at rest is different then when athletes are under stress. This will allow the body to train beyond its normal limits and prepare athletes to reproduce the same results when competing.

FLEXIBILITY

Flexibility is the ability of our joints and muscles to move through their full potential range of motion. It makes the body move more effectively and improves posture, alignment and physical appearance. When we speak of flexibility, it is important to differentiate between:

> ‣ **Mobility:** The potential range of motion available by the body in each joint.
>
> ‣ **Flexibility:** Neural control over mobility.

Our ability to move through our maximum range of motion is a combination of the **muscle fibres slowly gaining more tolerance before reaching breaking point** (just like an elastic band) and the **joints becoming more adaptable to support the added mobility.** The ability to be flexible will help to minimise the risk of injury. Sporting performance improves significantly because of a higher range of motion.

	Role in stretch	Stretch Factor	Danger
Ligament	Binds bone to bone inside a capsule, holds joint stability, should not be stretched.	Mobile, but very limited stretchability.	Excess stretching causes strain.
Tendon	Joins muscle to bone, holds the joint in position and secure stability.	Very stiff, almost no stretchability.	Tearing or lengthening causes a sprain.
Muscle fascia	Sticky tissue that envelops muscle fibres, providing structure to the muscle. It makes up 30% of a muscle's mass.	Fascia is very malleable and can be stretched safely. It contributes to a joint's range of motion by about 40%.	If the fascia is cold, mobility will be greatly reduced.
Muscle fibre	Relaxes	Very stretchy, can stretch to about 150% before tearing.	Muscle tear
Synovial fluid	Lubricates the joint	N/A	If cold, the synovial fluid cannot operate its function of lubrication.

Being flexible in cheerleading is essential (especially for flyers and tumblers). Fully understanding how stretching works goes far beyond just 'warming up' before training. The balance and timings are delicate, and lack of understanding of this science is what causes a large number of injuries in our sport.

Additionally, when stretching we are fighting the **stretch reflex.** The stretch reflex is when the nervous system automatically works against the stretch to regain control and stability of the joint to protect the muscles. Imagine yourself on an ice rink with slippers on: your legs will start to drift apart and you will instinctively try to bring your legs together without thinking about it. This is the stretch reflex and it's constantly working against us when we stretch. The more uncontrolled the stretch is, the more the stretch reflex will cause the muscle to contract.

Interestingly enough, the stretch reflex is not something we are born with. Babies bodies have not developed the ability to sense when a certain movement could potentially be dangerous. This is why they have a natural ability to do the splits and contort themselves in all sorts of shapes. Fast-forward eighty years, and the body has created a defence mechanism to avoid becoming injured, limiting mobility and flexibility almost entirely. Therefore we need to train against the stretch reflex to teach our nervous system that certain movements are safe for us to do, in addition to physically training our muscle fibres and joints to become more flexible.

Appropriate stretching before performing skills is needed to ensure the muscles have been brought to their maximum range of motion. This will prevent injuries during training and ensure that flexibility is maintained after the muscles have been contracted. The key is to follow these guidelines:

> ‣ **Stretching before cheer training should only be preparatory**, never developmental, as this will cause joints to become less stable and weaken muscle fibres, causing potential sprains, strains or dislocations. Preparatory stretches involve dynamic movements which pass through positions (e.g. high

kicks, side lunges), or basic held stretches, without exceeding the current range of motion.

‣ **Flexibility is the antagonist** (opposing) **movement of strength**, so a balance must be found in between.

‣ The **muscles should always be warm.** A 5-minute jog is just not enough to increase the body temperature by 1 or 2 degrees, which is required to make all the joints and muscle components develop a higher tolerance to the stretch.

‣ Athletes need to **stretch for at least 5 minutes at the end of every training** session in order to fully restore their muscles and work on developmental flexibility. Coaches and athletes who do not make time for stretching at the end of a session need to be aware that this will reduce their athlete's range of motion the following days, causing their skills to regress and risking a potential injury.

‣ For a stretch to be effective, it should be **held between 15 and 30 seconds**, and 2-4 repetitions of this are required.

‣ Use this **breathing** technique **effectively:** inhale deeply whilst relaxing the stretch, and exhale slowly whilst taking the stretch further.

‣ **To maintain flexibility,** stretch **2-3 times a week** minimum. Stretch **5-7 times a week to improve** flexibility.

There are four types of stretching techniques that can be used, each with their own specific function and suitability:

‣ **Static stretches:** Here you would use held positions with little or no movement. This is the safest way of developing short-term flexibility. Best used at the end of training so that if muscles cool down without the presence of movement, you won't need to rewarm them and you don't risk reducing explosiveness before training. Best used at the end of training by going beyond the range of motion and with good breathing technique, static stretches can be a great way to work on long-terms flexibility. With beginners who are still learning to control their movements, static stretches are a good option to get them familiar with stretching.

▸ **Dynamic stretches:** In this case, the stretch positions are performed with controlled movement to enhance the range of motion of the stretch. The movement also helps to keep the muscles warm. It's important to control the movement so that the stretches do not become ballistic. This can be used at the end of training for long-term flexibility or after warmup (as long as the athlete does not go beyond the range of motion).

▸ **PNF:** (Proprioceptive Neuromuscular Facilitation) This style of stretching works against the force of the muscles being contracted (usually with the aid of a partner, barre or exercise band). It's a highly efficient method for long-term flexibility and also makes great for partner work, but it should never be used before training skills so that power and joint stability is not lost. All levels can use this at the end of the session, but be mindful of basic safety precautions when using an external force to create a stretch.

▸ **Ballistic stretches:** Vigorous movements which allow a further range of motion. This type of exercise allows for little control as it uses the force of momentum to push the stretch so it can be dangerous when performed by inexperienced athletes. Advanced stretching like this should only be used by expert athletes, at the end of the session and never before training skills which require strength or power.

Athletes with limited flexibility will find it challenging to reach their full range of motion and may attempt to 'cheat' to achieve the stretch by bending limbs and arching the back. Dynamic stretches may turn into ballistic movements, as some athletes are less able to control their movements. To ensure they are stretching safely and effectively, use slow music, opt for static stretches, reinforce the breathing technique and encourage them to keep the correct form. Over-flexibility requires equal amounts of strengthening to ensure that the joints remain stable and safe to sustain the impact from tumbling, jumping and other cheerleading activities where the joints have the potential to be compromised.

MOTOR SKILLS

Motor fitness is a skill-related aspect of fitness, which encompasses agility, balance, speed, coordination, reaction time and power. Skilful movements are more energy-efficient and reduce the risk of injury. The *peripheral nervous system* (PNS) collects information via the sensory system, and then the central nervous system receives and processes this information, sending an appropriate response via the motor system.

Our muscles and nervous system have the ability to 'store' movement and execution to the point where the unconscious takes over conscious, deliberate action. This is the transition from the cognitive phase of learning into associative. Motor skills are developed through a number of factors:

> ‣ **Motor development:** Our ability to change our motor process though growth (physical) and maturation (functional).

> ‣ **Coordination:** Our ability to use different parts of our bodies for a smooth, controlled movement.

> ‣ **Sequential firing:** The ability of the nervous system to coordinate and activate muscles to contract in a sequential order throughout the kinetic chain.

> ‣ **Procedural memory:** The long-term memory that embeds the way we perform motor actions.

> ‣ **Reactivity of the kinetic chain:** The ability of all parts of our bodies (muscles, joints, nerves) working together to produce movements.

When teaching a new skill or section of choreography, it should be broken down into bite-sized elements so that the motor system can sequentially process the information. If necessary, you can teach arm and leg elements separately and then combine them to learn the full sequence. With practice and repetition, the coordination will become smoother, quicker and more precise until the skill is performed autonomously with good technique.

Even with progressions in mind, a "throw it and fix it later" approach to technique has been widespread in cheerleading, especially with newer or grassroots cheer communities. Sadly, this only reinforces poor muscle memory which is almost impossible to reverse and is more detrimental than not learning the skill at all. The consequences affected by repetition of poor technique include:

- More time spent to get rid of bad habits (procedural memory is extremely difficult to reverse).
- Getting good at doing something bad something that is not useful - SAID Principle.
- Poor scores from performing poor technique in competition.
- Difficulty in progressing to harder skills.
- Risk of injury even at current ability level due to incorrect body alignment during impact, especially when athlete is suffering muscle fatigue. This is why, for example, it is not recommended to use skills such as a back-handspring as a method of conditioning unless the technique is consistent throughout the drill. The risk of developing incorrect long-term muscle memory outweighs the advantages of skill-specific conditioning. Of course, skills have to be trained under 'full out' conditions (i.e. over 80% heart rate and with at least 2 minutes of muscle fatigue). Otherwise, the training will be almost useless on the competition floor. Ensuring technique is consistent when the skill is executed in a 'full out' is the safest way to protect athletes from injury and to avoid deductions on the score sheets.

NUTRITION

Nutrition is one of those subjects that can open a can of worms. The subject is extensive, but understanding the fundamental principles of nutrition is an important element of being an efficient cheerleading coach or athletes. This nutrition section outlines these basic principles for everyday use, and I highly recommend reading *The Cheer Diet* by Coach Sahil M. for more in-depth understanding.

NUTRITION ISSUES IN CHEERLEADING

In cheerleading, we mainly see three key issues:

1. **Junk Food:** Eating this in excess is completely counterproductive to all other efforts, and even though each athlete needs to pay attention to the amount of energy they require, the source of energy is also important. It's rather obvious that 100 calories of chocolate is not as beneficial as 100 calories of oats. Food serves a much more specific function than just providing energy. What we eat affects our hormones, body performance, energy levels, muscle building, etc.

2. **Under-eating/crash diets:** Cutting out one group of foods completely and/or starving oneself is dangerous. Eating too little too frequently can have a negative impact on the metabolism and more importantly, proper energy production. You'll also have weaker muscular contractions on a big calorie deficit - so stunts will drop and tumbling will be slower.

3. **Over-eating:** Some athletes overcompensate or overestimate for the type of exercise and calorie expenditure. They believe that they can eat as much as they want 'because they're exercising'. This is another issue that they need to be aware of in order to maintain their athletic ability.

As a matter of priority, these three areas are the first we need to address to help cheerleaders and parents who may be actively inhibiting their performance potential. As it's been said, you can't out-train a bad diet, so none of the training efforts in all other areas are going to have an impact if cheerleaders keep fuelling their efforts with unhealthy eating habits. We are not saying that cheerleaders need to stop enjoying life and become obsessed with the idea of nutrition, but they must understand the basic principles of nutrition and how they affect their overall performance.

NOTE: What people refer to as a 'calorie' is technically incorrect - the official term is 'kilocalories' (i.e. 1000 calories) - so what we refer to as a '200-calorie' doughnut should really be referred to as a '200-kilocalorie doughnut (i.e. 200kcal). As this is such a technical term, it has become accepted within our culture to simply use the word 'calorie'. In this book, the term 'calorie' is used instead of 'kilocalorie'.

FOOD GROUPS & USES

There are six primary categories of nutrients: carbohydrates, lipids (fats), proteins, vitamins, minerals and water, which can be classified into two groups: *macronutrients* (those that we need a lot of and give us energy: carbs, fats, proteins, water) and *micronutrients* (those that we need in smaller quantities: vitamins and minerals).

Food Type	Use	Examples	Notes
Carbohydrates	Energy: *complex carbs* (slow, sustainable release) and *simple carbs* (fast release but causes a spike and crash)	*Complex*: Brown rice, oats, whole grain, vegetables *Simple*: Bread, pasta, chocolate, sugars	Carbohydrates are REQUIRED for sports performance. It's worth noting that not all carbohydrates are the same and there are some severe pitfalls.
Proteins	Growth, maintenance and repair of the body (muscles, cell membranes, immune defences, bones), minor contribution to energy	Chicken, beef, tofu, lentils, beans	Protein is essential for a balanced diet and sports performance. It doesn't hurt to be aware of animal cruelty and exploitation and try to opt for responsibly-sourced animal products
Vitamins & Minerals	Critical role in metabolism: ~~they~~ help enzymes work more efficiently	FRESH fruits & vegetables	There is no better place than getting these from nature: eat whole foods!
Fats	Energy, brain cell development + hair, nails, skin health, vitamin absorption, hormone function	Vegetable oils, butter, cream, animal fat, fish oil	Good fats are essential to our diet. See the section *'Recommendations for Cheerleaders'*
Water	Solvent, transport medium, lubricant, regulates body temperature	Also present in soups, juices, vegetables with high water content	Makes up 60% of the volume your body can dehydrate even with a 2% fluctuation

MANAGING BODY EXPECTATIONS

As coaches, we have to ensure we are enhancing our athlete's performance potential by ensuring they are healthy, but we also need to protect them from developing unrealistic expectations and eating disorders. We can do this by choosing language that will avoid any reference to weight and looks, focusing instead on fitness performance which has nothing to do with a person's physique. We can further help athletes manage expectations by helping them understand these basic principles:

1) There are three body types, which are determined by our genetics. All males and females will fall somewhere on the spectrum, and knowing our dominant type is helpful so that we can adjust our nutrition and training methods accordingly.

- **Ectomorphs:** Those that find it hard to gain either muscle or fat, and usually have long, thin physiques with a higher proportion of slow-twitch muscles.

- **Mesomorphs:** Those that gain both muscle and fat mass easily, depending on their eating and training habits.

- **Endomorphs:** Those who gain fat more easily than muscle.

Ectomorph	Mesomorph	Endomorph

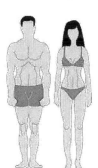 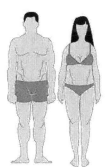

- Narrow hips & clavicles
- Small joints (wrists / ankles)
- Thin build
- Stringy ab muscles
- Long Limbs
- Predominantly slow-twitch

- Wide clavicles
- Narrow waist
- Thinner joints
- Long, round abs
- More fast-twitch

- Blocky
- Thick rib cage
- Wide / thicker joints
- Hips as wide as clavicle
- Shorter limbs
- Balanced fast and slow twitch muscles

2) Weight should not be a measure of body image. In equal volume, muscle weighs more than fat. In comparative terms, 1 litre of muscle weighs 2.3 pounds, while 1 litre of fat weighs 1.98 pounds. This is why I never recommend using BMI or weight as a measure of fitness or body image. Instead, body fat percentage is used as a more accepted method of measurement. Females have a naturally higher percentage than men. The accepted guidelines for male and female fat percentages are:

	Women	Men
Essential (vital) fat	10-13%	2-5%
Professional athletes	14-20%	6-13%
Athletic standard	21-24%	14-17%
Average for non athletes	25-31%	18-24%
Obese	32%+	25%+

3) Body shape is caused by a combination of genetics and hormones. The body shape (e.g. pear, apple, hourglass, etc) will be different for every person, in addition to their body type. This is partly due to the genetic code but also to the hormone imbalances someone may have (caused by nutrition, stress levels, thyroid, the contraceptive pill, and many other factors). It is important for athletes to accept that the way they are built genetically is not something that they can change. However, they may be interested in knowing that certain traits (such as having a disproportionate amount of fat accumulated on the hips) could be a result of a hormonal imbalance that is worth checking with a medical practitioner.

The main hormones linked that affect the body's shape and response to nutrition are:

- **Leptin:** Secreted from fat cells to the brain after you start your meal, signals the body that you are full. It is released by chewing, so the more you chew the fuller you will feel.

- **Ghrelin:** Made in the gut, it signals hunger to the body. The bigger the volume and frequency of meals are, the more ghrelin is secreted in between meals to signal hunger.

- **Adiponectin:** Enhances your body's ability to use carbohydrates for energy. The lower the body fat percentage, the more this is released.

- **Insulin:** Regulates your blood sugar levels when eating high glycemic index foods. Insulin helps store carbs and build fat.

- **Glucagon:** Works against insulin to burn down carbs and fat to be used as energy.

- **CCK:** Released when eating fats and proteins and signals the body that you are full. Released slowly so you feel fuller for a longer period of time.

- **Human Growth Hormone (HGH):** Helps build muscle and break down fat cells. It is released through intense exercise and the more muscle the body has.

- **Sex hormones (Oestrogen, progesterone, testosterone):** Affect the release of other hormones.

4) Cardio, strength training and diet balance. Achieving an optimal physical condition requires a balance of cardio, strength training and diet. Avoiding any one of these three elements will inhibit an athlete's ability to achieve the results they are looking for. Omitting strength training (by dieting and cardio training only) will result in a weak and limp physique. Not paying attention to diet (cardio and strength training only) won't yield the desired results and make the fat loss process almost impossible. Lastly, avoiding cardio (strength training and diet only) may not be enough to trigger fat loss, even if muscle mass is improved.

5) First to stay is last to go. Expanding on the point above, some people may find it frustrating that the fat accumulated in certain parts "doesn't seem to budge" no matter how healthy they are eating or how much they exercise. This is what is known as 'stubborn fat'. What is important to understand is that fat is not equally distributed: the body shape will be determined by where the genes and hormones are telling the fat to be 'anchored.' The body thinks: "in case I starve, this is the most efficient place to store my backup fuel, so I will make sure to keep it safe there". This is why the first place we put fat on will be the last to go and the reason why most people give up, thinking there is no progress.

At times, this causes the figure to look disproportionate because, even though the body is leaning out in some areas, the stubborn fat clings onto other areas. This can be frustrating especially to those who don't understand that this evens out later in the fat loss process. For example: a pear-shaped female on a diet will notice that her waist and arms have slimmed down but that her thighs are still the same size. This might make her thighs look even wider, because it's now in disproportion with her slimming waist (which is not an area of stubborn fat for their body type). This is why it's important look at how clothes fit or body fat percentage rather than scales to monitor progress.

6) 1st Law of Thermodynamics. Energy can be transformed from one form to another but cannot be created or destroyed. Calories consumed will replenish the calories used. Eating fewer calories will create a deficit, eating more will cause excess to be stored in fat cells.

7) Quality versus quantity. The quality of the calories consumed is also important because nutrients serve a specific function. For example, 800 calories of popcorn versus 800 calories of a balanced meal of fish, greens and rice will have two complete different effects in the way that the body uses this energy.

Sweets have no useful nutrients and minerals, so the body will keep 'looking for' nutrition, meaning you are likely to still be hungry and eat more than what's necessary. Imagine yourself eating a tub of ice-cream versus a tub of vegetables and let's say you like broccoli just as much as you like ice-cream (yeah right!). You will find it very easy to eat all the ice-cream because it has no nutritional value, so your brain will not get the 'stop eating, you have fuelled up enough' signals. In contrast, when eating broccoli your body will be much quicker at sending these signals to the brain due to its high nutritional value. This is why nutritional value is so important to our meals: it's not just about how many calories we eat but also how much they contribute to our system and help us self-regulate and avoid over-eating.

GUIDELINES FOR ATHLETES & PARENTS

When we are not qualified nutritionists, it can be difficult to give athletes dietary recommendations. The following guidelines were written as concepts that can be shared with cheerleaders and parents in mind without needing a significant amount of nutritional background. I will also warn that the nutrition aspect of fitness is one that can lead us down some odd rabbit holes, and there is a whole industry dedicated to scare-mongering and developing an obsession with nutrition. As with everything, balance is key and most often than not, the "Keep It Simple" principle is the best to follow. After all, we don't see the rest of the animal species over thinking their nutrition, and I can't think of any of them having the same weight-related issues that we humans do. However, I do think that getting a basic nutritional understanding is very useful for coaches, parents and athletes, especially in regards to sports performance, which is why I can highly recommend *The Cheer Diet* by coach Sahil M.

In this chapter, I touch upon the basics which are necessary for all coaches and athletes to be aware of. In terms of implementing them the basics, it is understandable that in some countries and areas of the world, they will be easier to follow than in others. Different communities have distinctive customs and easier access to whole foods (ie food in their most natural form) in comparison to areas where processed foods and ready meals are more readily available.

For now, try to read these guidelines with an open mind away from your culture, the current contents of your refrigerator, your usual shopping list and any fears or opinions. The guidelines below are simple, healthy, instructive and constructive to create the best athlete possible: with a sharp mind and a body fit for the sport we love.

DITCH THE SCALES

Scales belong in the kitchen to weigh ingredients. Scales are dangerous and misleading because:

> ‣ Muscle is denser than fat: a cup of muscle weighs more than a cup of fat, and muscle is more valuable since it's active tissue.
> ‣ Weight fluctuates depending on the time of day, month, etc.
> ‣ When looking at scales, you see a number and you can attach an emotion to the number. You are likely to have negative feelings towards the numbers regardless of what they are. Let's be honest, how many people go onto the scale, and say "YAY!"
> ‣ It can become a dangerous obsession with numbers.

Instead of scales, get yourself two pairs of jeans. The first is in the size you currently are and the second is your next target size (a size up or a size down, depending on what your goal is).

The style of jeans is as important as the size. Make sure that you're picking a style that goes with your body shape. Try both pairs of jeans on once a week or once a fortnight and measure your progress that way. *It's about how you feel* in your jeans that's important, not the numbers on the scale. Take a picture of your progress and repeat the process until you have reached a healthy goal.

80:20 RULE

It's not expected that you follow these rules 100% of the time. You are not training for the Olympics (yet!). Before cheer, there is also your life (even though at times it may seem that cheer *IS* life). If you are able to follow these rules 80% of the time, you will be on an excellent track, and you will see some incredible results in your performance. Shift to 70/30% when you're on holiday or 90/10 if you feel you need an extra boost. Whatever you do, make sure you never fall below 60/40 to avoid damaging your health and athletic potential.

CARBS ARE ESSENTIAL FOR SPORT

When you hear "you shouldn't eat carbs" it can be confusing because it is a contradiction for athletes. "You shouldn't eat carbs" is true when we want to maximise burning fat, but if you're training to compete, not eating carbs is completely counterproductive. Carbs are energy and muscles require energy to function. There are two options to get energy: by consuming glycogen or from your body's fat stores. Studies have shown that getting energy from fat will slow the muscles down by an average of 20-30%. To perform to the best ability, the right carbohydrates need to be eaten at strategic times. For example, eating complex carbohydrates a few hours before warm up or competition so that the glycogen is in the blood stream when it's needed will be turn it into rocket fuel. As with everything, balance is key and we need to make sure we are eating enough carbohydrates to support our athletic endeavours. We also need to make sure we are exercising enough to prevent excess calories being stored as fat.

Good examples of carbohydrate-heavy foods that can still be healthy for sports are: pasta with fresh tomato sauce, raw vegetables, regular or sweet potatoes, rice.

LOW GI VS HIGH GI CARBS

It needs to be stressed that not all carbs are the same. They each have a distinctive chemistry and different glycemic index (GI). This is a rating system that is used to describe a food's potential to raise the blood sugar and insulin levels in our bodies. A high GI food (such as an energy drink or chocolate bar) will cause a sugar rush (insulin spike) and a crash (feeling sleepy or headache). A low GI food will release energy more slowly and steadily (whole grain bread) without causing a spike. Low GI foods are much better for sports than high GI, unless of course there is the need to cause a rapid spike (such as someone feeling faint just before competing).

In general, it is best to reduce as much refined sugar and white carbs as possible. These have a high GI, are not beneficial to our health or immune system, plus they lower metabolism and have no nutritional value whatsoever. Sugar is an inflammatory chemical that can make illnesses worse and it has been proven to be as addictive as heroin. Sugars need to be seen as 'treats' instead of being part of a daily regimen. Nowadays, we are lucky to have alternative natural sweeteners such as Stevia or Xylitol that are great for replacing or complementing sugar in recipes (for example, using two thirds of the sugar required and replace the rest with a natural sweetener).

Eat more: Vegetables, whole grain, oats, sweet potatoes, beans, lentils, fruits. **Avoid:** Added sugar, milk chocolate, white chocolate, candy, cakes, energy drinks, fruit juice & smoothies (unless they are made fresh), high sugar breakfast cereals, energy bars, granola, etc... Always check sugar or sodium content on the back label. **Tip:** In many states in the USA (especially in the South), sugar finds its way into everything, even vegetables! In restaurants, make sure you ask for no added sugar on your food.

ADD MORE PROTEIN

Eating the right amount of lean protein, such as chicken, fish, turkey or tofu, will help build muscle. Pork, beef and other animal products are still protein; just be mindful of the fat content. It's important to include some form of protein in every meal. An easy way to do this is snacking on beef, turkey or ostrich biltong (or low sugar beef jerky), chicken, shrimp or poached eggs with asparagus or spinach. You can also add nutritional supplements such as protein bars and shakes, just check the contents as many of them have enough sugar and chemicals in them to do as much bad as good. Just remember that nothing is as good for you as what nature provides. If you're a vegetarian, ensure you are getting your protein from soy, nuts and other products - and in enough quantities. Athletes need more protein than non-athletes, especially when training long hours.

Eat more: Chicken (KFC does not count!) beef, turkey, beans, lentils, soy (females only as excess soy for males can cause issues), tofu, eggs, whey (protein in milk), nuts.

KNOW YOUR DRINKS

The body is made up of 60-70% water. By not drinking enough water (just a 2% decrease) we will start to suffer the side effects of dehydration: headaches, dizziness, fainting, muscles will lose speed and strength. Water is always the best option but occasionally we like to have something different. Not all drinks are the same, and the important thing is to know what's in them before we choose them.

Energy drinks, frappuccinos, 'fat free' beverages, syrups, fruit juices and sports drinks are laden with sugar. Not only will this be detrimental in an effort to lower body fat, it will also cause a huge spike in blood sugar due to the high glycemic index. It's best to replace these with infused water (peppermint, strawberry or any other flavoured tea bag). For sport, coconut water is an excellent source of electrolytes. Replenishing potassium levels is key to avoiding cramps, so eating a banana before training can replace the need for a sugary sports drink. Diet beverages may seem like a clever choice but the body finds it difficult to break down the chemicals which replace the sugar. This could inhibit digestion, metabolism, the ability to lose fat and pose more significant long-term health issues.

GOOD VERSUS BAD FATS

There's a reason why, on average, Mediterranean people live longer than anyone else: they have very little bad fats in their diet, little sugar and it is mainly based on what nature provides. There is much debate and controversy around whether some fats are good or bad. For example, many health campaigns in the past have warned us against saturated fats, but coconut oil, a saturated fat, has been proven to reduce cholesterol and has other beneficial properties. The words FAT FREE are not always the right answer. Most of the time it's just a clever marketing trick. What food companies don't tell you is that to make up for the taste and texture fat provides, they throw in tons of sugar, corn syrup, gums and chemicals. The top 5 oils for a healthy diet, in moderation, are:

- Virgin coconut oil: Extensive amount of nutrients, antioxidants and health benefits.
- Macadamia oil: Good for cooking at high temperatures, nutty taste.
- Fish oil: Full of Omega 3 and 6, great for the heart and a sharper brain.
- Virgin olive oil: Full of antioxidants, perfect for drizzling and best used cold.
- Light olive oil: Ideal for cooking at high temperatures, neutral taste.

Avoid: Processed cheese, fried foods, anything containing palm oil, lard, shortening. **Tip:** Instead of opting for 'fat free' products which are full of sugar and chemicals, go for 'half fat' instead as these are much healthier overall.

DRINK BEFORE YOU EAT

The body doesn't differentiate between hunger and thirst, so learning how to distinguish the two is important. Unless the conditions are extreme (on a really hot day, if you are dehydrated or just after exercise), you can't really tell the difference between the signals. Here is how you can tell if it's hunger or thirst:

1. At the first signs of hunger, drink a glass of water. Wait 15 minutes.

2. If you're still hungry after 15 minutes, eat a small handful of almonds (make sure you're not doing this too many times a day because the calories quickly add up) or an apple. Nuts are really satisfying due to their protein and fat content and require lots of chewing (which helps to release leptin) and have a very low glycemic index. Apples are full of fibre and they'll help fill up your stomach in a short time. They are a great way to curb hunger pangs for longer and give you instant satisfaction and nutrition.

3. If you're still hungry after 20 minutes, it means it was real hunger and it's time for a meal. A 35-minute wait won't have changed your life but it can significantly help you with your hunger management in the future.

BOYCOTT PROCESSED AND JUNK FOODS

There is a long list of why processed foods are so bad for you. Humans are not meant to eat all these things. The body protects itself by bloating, becoming ill, gaining fat. Think about this: how many sick or overweight animals can be found in nature? Unless they have been affected by man (through pollution, captivity, etc.) the answer is almost none. Nature takes care of itself and living beings have been doing fine since the beginning of time. Enter processed, refined and junk foods, and the human race has forgotten how to take care of itself. The reasons these foods are so bad for us are:

- ‣ **Most contain palm oil.** Unlike coconut oil which is very good for you, this is a cheap, horrible oil made from palm fruit. Sadly it's in almost any food that comes in a box.
- ‣ **Sugar and chemicals are added to make food last longer.** These additives are addictive and cause hidden fat gain and also a variety of illnesses because due to inflammation.
- ‣ **Excess sodium is added for taste.** Food manufacturers add sodium to hide the taste of the sugar and preservatives added in the food. Sodium is very dangerous if you eat too much of it (table salt and what they add to processed foods is not the same. Salt is only 40% sodium).
- ‣ **They're addictive.** These products are made so that you become addicted to them. Many of the ingredients (like hidden sugar content) will cause addiction-like reactions such as insatiable cravings and even withdrawals.

It might be convenient to buy a frozen ready meal, but consider this: unless it was made naturally by our planet, we are not designed to eat it. The human body can cope with it, but it's not what we are made for. Eating an excess of foods that are not natural increases the likelihood of a number of short-term and long-term health issues. If we attempt to eat like nature intended it won't take long to see that making tasty, quick alternatives is much easier than we think.

You can pack an omelette or a burrito wrap with your favourite chopped vegetables and protein. Sautéd fish in a pan with olive oil, salt and lemon (later joined by vegetables) requires just one pan and a few minutes: it's a staple mediterranean meal. Cooked shrimp or salmon tossed in seasoned baby spinach leaves and tomatoes makes a delicious, hearty salad. Wraps are nutritious, light, and you can put anything you want in them whilst avoiding processed food 'junk'. It's not that hard to make the right choices, but it all starts at the supermarket.

Avoid: All fast food, canned food, breakfast cereal, pre-made food, frozen meals. **Choose:** Anything made by planet earth. Learn how to pair them and season them to your taste. **Tip:** Shop around the edges where the food is fresh. Stay out of the aisles full of bags and boxes.

TREAT MEAL

Good news: you don't need to be strict ALL the time. A treat meal a week (not a full day) is not only recommended but also necessary to keep your metabolism guessing. This is the '20' of the 80/20 rule mentioned previously. Including one treat meal a week to reward yourself with your favourite foods is a great way to boost metabolism and ensure that leptin levels stay optimised. If you're too good all the time, your body might start to defend itself by lowering the metabolic rate and clinging onto fat stores for energy in prevention for malnourishment.

This means that consistent diligence with your nutrition can cause plateaus and plateaus will make it more difficult for you to burn fat. It's best to plan your treat meals ahead so that it's something to look forward to. Of course, it's 'treat meal', not 'treat week'! Remember the following ratios: 80/20 is normal, 70/30 on holidays and – 90/10 if you want to give yourself an extra boost.

MIND AND FOCUS

Enabling the mind to be focused and prepared for athletic activity is just as important as having adequate skill and physical conditioning. If an athlete is attempting to execute a skill with any slight doubt, it can have a detrimental effect and potentially become the root of a mental block. As coaches it is important to understand how the mental aspect of competitive cheer can affect the overall performance and skill development.

WHITE HORSE THINKING

Close your eyes and think of anything, but don't think of a black horse. What did you think of? Most likely some sort of black Beauty galloping into the wind. Beautiful as that stallion may be, the objective of the exercise was to *not* think of a black horse. Wouldn't it be simpler to ask someone to think of something (like a white horse) instead of *not* thinking of something (like the black horse)? Of course it would be, yet our industry is plagued with 'Black Horse' coaching, focused on criticism and what not to do rather than positive reinforcement:

- Don't bend your legs.
- Stop bailing out.
- Don't sit in your cradle.

We would do well to make this style of coaching obsolete in the years to come. It is encouraging to see more and more teams being coached with *white horse thinking*: giving specific, positive instructions and corrections:

- Straighten your leg / push your knee back.
- Set your mind to complete the skill.
- Whip your hips forward.

White horse thinking also needs to be executed carefully or it can have the opposite effect. If you heard "Think of a white horse with top-knotted braided hair, a Somerset saddle, oiled hooves, running on a rainy day on the coast of southern France," you may stop paying attention before you hear the end of the sentence. Worse yet, you could get stuck on what a 'Somerset saddle' is and not hear the rest at all. You may even forget to think of your white horse altogether.

Instead, you would want to hear the most important details first. Add one detail at a time once you are more comfortable. The same can be said with how you instruct your athletes. If there are ten corrections to be made, start with the most important instructions before drilling the skill more. Then add one detail at a time until the athlete is comfortable keeping and executing all corrections together.

MINDSET

Mindset explains why some athletes are able to withstand challenges throughout their career and still succeed, while other athletes end up not being able to scratch the surface of their potential despite their seemingly unlimited talent.

Mindset is a simple yet revolutionary idea, developed by Stanford Psychologist Dr. Carol Dweck. Mindset explains why talent alone does not equal success and often times, stands in the way of success. Dweck and her team have been researching achievement and success over the last three decades and they have found that praising an athlete's talent or ability rather than increasing their self-esteem actually hinders it growth and achievement. Dr. Dweck names two types of mindset:

'FIXED MINDSET ATHLETES

- **Belief:** Their talent, ability and intelligence is limited or fixed (they only have a certain amount).

- **Tendency:** Constantly scan their environment, documenting how much talent they have or are perceived to have.

- **Success:** Believe that talent is what leads to success, so when they don't succeed, it means they are not talented.

- **Challenges:** Avoid challenges because they fear what it means to fail.

- **Effort:** Their effort is strong when they are doing well, but diminishes when they struggle.

GROWTH MINDSET ATHLETES

- **Belief:** Their basic traits can be developed and improved through hard work, dedication and perseverance.

- **Tendency:** See challenges as an opportunity to learn and grow, rather than a representation of how good or bad they are at something.

- **Success:** See success as something that is based on improvement, not winning.

- **Challenges:** Embraced and seen as a vital step in the process to improvement.

- **Effort:** Believe effort is the single most important element that will lead to their success.

PRAISING ATHLETES

Knowing how to praise athletes correctly is going to hugely help their mindset. Even though all praise may seem positive, you need to be aware of two very different types:

- ‣ **Ability praise:** Complimenting athletes on their talent, e.g. "You're such a gifted flyer."
- ‣ **Effort praise:** Complimenting athletes on their hard work and effort, e.g. "You worked really hard to get that scale, I'm proud of you."

Though at times the two types of praise sound virtually identical, they have exceptionally different impacts on an athlete. In more than thirty years of research on praise, Dr. Dweck and her colleagues found that when there is an overemphasis on talent or ability, we leave our athletes vulnerable to failure, fearful of challenges, and obsessed with looking good rather than working hard (Fixed Mindset).

Even though 'ability praise' is extremely well intentioned, it leads athletes down the wrong path. It keeps children focused on wanting to prove themselves through success. Sounds great, right? Unfortunately, it's counterproductive.

Imagine an athlete is constantly being told that they are gifted or phenomenal. Everything seems to be going for them as they continue to practice, trying to prove that they are worthy of that praise, until something stands in the way of that compliment. Maybe it's a fall during a routine, struggling with a new tumbling skill when they had previously learned everything with ease, or something as insignificant as not being in the front of the formation during the routine. For a child with a fixed mindset these situations become unbearable as they become representative of who they are as an athlete. They now see themselves as inept, no longer as talented or gifted. In contrast, athletes who are praised with a focus on effort and hard work can embrace challenges, concentrate on what they can control, and immerse themselves in their own skills rather than comparing themselves to others.

Another aspect to be mindful of is the way in which we present the praise: by putting the athlete at the centre of the action rather than in a passive position. For example: "I loved seeing you try your best" puts *yourself* at the centre of the action, while the athlete's action is passive. "You really were trying your best, well done" puts them directly in the centre of the praise action.

COACH'S RESPONSIBILITY

Telling an athlete they are talented or focusing on how fast they have attained a skill is counterproductive, but that doesn't mean we should not praise our cheerleaders. Instead,

- Praise your athletes for their hard work: *"You never gave up and kept fighting. I'm proud of you for working hard."*

- Focus on the steps that an athlete takes to achieving a skill: *"I noticed how you focused on improving your hurdle in those drills and then went and applied that to your round off tuck and it worked! Great work!"*

- Point out the hurdles that an athlete overcame to get to where they are: *"I'm so proud of how that fall in the stunt section didn't shake your confidence when going into your basket toss section. You nailed the rest of your routine. Way to push through."*

- Emphasise effort over anything else in practice: *"How many of you gave 100% effort in that full out? That's what I am talking about! That's how we are going to meet our goals, by always giving everything we've got."*

- Highlight when an athlete or team is improving, rather than focusing on perfection: *"I love how you continue to improve the height of your jumps. I can see how those strengthening exercises are gradually bringing your legs up to level."*

- To train mentally tough athletes it takes knowledge, insight, and deliberate actions from a coach. We know that praising a child is important, but the way we praise them is even more important for their development and future success.

VISUALISATION

Visualisation (or mental rehearsal) in elite sports has been around for decades. Billie Jean King used it in the 1960s when playing tennis and Gabby Douglas attributed it to her success as a three-time Olympic gold medalist in gymnastics. Visualisation is the process of creating a mental image of what you want to happen and how you want to feel while doing it. The use of visualisation prepares the muscles for action, aids in using proper technique, and conditions the mind to react to pressure.

There are many ways to use mental imagery in cheerleading. Athletes can use it for relaxation (to picture a peaceful place where they have no fears and no worries), success (to picture performing the ideal routine), to play out possible scenarios and how they will adapt, and/or to help with athletic rehabilitation after injury. Scientists have found that this mental rehearsal of imagery creates a blueprint in the brain and triggers neural firing in the muscles. Some studies show that imagery and visualisation simulate almost identical muscle action and neural firing as one would notice if they were performing the actual skill!

There are two main types of mental rehearsal: *internal imagery* and *external imagery.* With internal imagery, you see yourself performing a skill through your own eyes, as if you were there carrying out the skill. In external imagery, you see yourself as a spectator would. Both methods have validity, however, sports psychologists have mentioned that with the advancement in technology and the increased use of video equipment in training, external imagery is best used for practice time and internal imagery for competition.

One of the most popular techniques used for internal imagery is creating an imagery script. This is a very detailed account of each step of the competition process, from walking into the arena to meet your team, to stepping foot in the warm-up room and then all the way through to the end of your routine. Many psychologists suggest continuing the imagery script to the awards ceremony, picturing the outcome that you desire.

Using as many of your senses as possible to create a thorough and complete picture of the competition process (seeing the image and picture, feeling the muscles stretch and contract, hearing the beat of the music or roar of the crowd, touching the coarseness of the blue floor) is known to prepare yourself both mentally and physically.

Visualisation is not only helpful during competition time, but also after an injury. Scientists have found that mental imagery has been helpful in aiding injured athletes to heal faster (Ievleva and Orlick, 1999).

Mental imagery is not always as easy as it seems. Those athletes who had a more vivid and active imagination as young children have been seen to gravitate more easily towards visualisation. Children who did not or those who have experienced traumatic sports injuries or distressing misses often have a more difficult time with imagery. It's important for athletes to note that if they begin to see failure, a fall, or negative experience, they must stop, rewind and begin again, replaying the image until they see a successful scenario.

Guided imagery, visualisation and mental rehearsal can improve performance and productiveness in an athlete's training. During competitions, visualisation can be a great way to gain that competitive advantage every team and athlete is looking for.

MENTAL BLOCKS

Fear is a primal human emotion. Since the dawn of man, we have been programmed to fear anything that might pose a threat to our well being. Our survival instincts, often triggered by fear, instruct us to protect ourselves from imminent dangers. Mental blocks, the cheerleading equivalent of a survival instinct, can be caused by a variety of issues or 'stress factors' such as performing in front of an audience, attempting a tumbling skill without a spotter or even something imaginary. Whatever the source of the problem, the main issue is that the athlete gives into the fear. Over time, that fear can build and, left without proper attention or guidance, the athlete may develop a mental block. Isolating the 'fear factor' (identifying the culprit and the severity of the issue) before it becomes a mental block is essential before helping an athlete overcome the issue.

STRESS

Stress may come from issues with personal life, anxiety, poor nutrition or many other factors. If this seems to be the principal cause of the mental block, the athlete should take time to relax physically and mentally before performing. The main cause of stress may need to be brought to the attention of a parent or professional as this may extend outside of your role.

FEAR OF INJURY

Fear of injury is the most plausible reason for mental blocks. It is important to note that fear of injury can stem from a variety of factors like experiencing an injury previously, witnessing an injury or simply recognising that injury is possible. The one positive aspect of this type of block is that we can clearly understand why it exists, so steps can be taken to build the athlete up. With this type of mental block, the physical 'fail' needs to be addressed and conditioned beyond the point of confidence so that before they attempt the skill, athletes are fully aware of what could cause an injury and why this will not happen to them this time. If an athlete had been injured previously, coaches should investigate the reasons why the injury happened.

Most of these can be narrowed down to a weak area of the body that sustained a force greater than what it is capable of withstanding; therefore, conditioning to reinforce the area WILL solve the problem. The goal is for the athlete to fully acknowledge, in a form such as this one: "I landed badly on my back tuck and sprained my ankle because it was too weak to sustain the impact. I have now spent a month building strength in my ankles and I know they can sustain more force on impact than my back tuck is willing to give it." With this kind of outlook, the athlete should be mentally ready to train and perform skills after completing a full course of rehab to the injury.

SELF-SABOTAGE

Some athletes turn to self-sabotage for fear of failure. This may sound contradicting, but by self-sabotaging their skill they are taking control over their failure. We see examples of this everywhere; in people who are dieting but sabotage themselves with a binge-session before their final weigh-in or a student deciding to abandon the books and attend a party the night before an important exam. In cheer, it may be translated to someone on the team being scared that they are not good enough in comparison to their teammates, or that they may not be able to progress after this one skill is mastered.

The best way of tackling this mental block is by relieving the mental pressure of their achievements and leaving them the head space to get back into the saddle. If you are closer to competition, this may mean that you remove that skill or ask the athlete to perform a lower skill. This may seem like a dangerous tactic that will affect your score, but athletes are more likely to hit the skill and rebuild confidence if pressure is relieved temporarily.

LOW CONFIDENCE

Low confidence comes from the simple fact that the athlete does not believe their body is capable of doing said skill. While the athlete's assessment of their abilities might be correct, they need to be shown that their body can do each skill in isolation. They will also need enough repetition until the skill becomes muscle memory. Tackling the physical demands of the skill individually (strength, power, speed, flexibility and motor ability) will give them physical evidence that they are able to complete the skill safely.

ATTENTION-SEEKING

Unfortunately, the epidemic of mental blocks tends to spread as an attention-seeking method, whether it is conscious or subconscious. If this is the known reason for the block, it may be best to ignore the athlete's complaints and only pay attention by rewarding positive behaviour. Just like children who develop tantrums because it is the only time they get attention from their parents (even if it is negative), serial "mental blockists" are only really crying out for recognition. There is nothing wrong with this as long as the recognition is positive and all other behaviour is ignored or dealt with using a passive form of discipline.

GREAT EXPECTATIONS

"I've missed more than 9000 shots in my career. I've lost almost 300 games. 26 times, I've been trusted to take the game-winning shot and missed. I've failed over and over and over again in my life. And that is why I succeed."

Michael Jordan

One thing I've realised by being exposed to an extremely varied and international cheerleading community is that within the world of competitive cheer, we are exposed to two bipolar realities:

REALITY A: On one side of the spectrum, we see cheer teams adding skills to their routines which are way above their capabilities. In some communities, "hitting zero"(performing a routine with zero deductions) is almost unobtainable. It is generally accepted that hitting a full out clean routine can be considered a miracle: it's great when it happens but generally not expected. The expectation is so low that we fail to push our abilities.

REALITY B: In another reality, the pressure of NOT hitting is not just a shame, it's a disaster. Teams are expected to "hit zero" and if things don't go the way they are expected to, we see utterly devastated coaches or athletes taking the weight of the world on their shoulders. The expectation is so high that we fail unless we reach the top.

You may be reading Reality A or Reality B and wondering if this actually happens. Yes. Competitive cheer lives in two separate realities, unfortunately, both of which are damaging to our athletes and our sport. Managing expectations (from the coach, parent, team, individual and crowd perspective) within cheer is far from being consistent. Add to this the myriad of scoring sheets from different event producers, making it difficult to define a realistic range of expectations. What are the problems created by the expectations in Reality A vs Reality B?

REALITY A challenges:

- Promotes a poor athlete progression arch which can lead to bad technique, insufficient conditioning, more injuries and other bad habits.

- Athletes are pushed beyond their capabilities, encouraging a lack of consistency and technique which results in poor execution.

- It fully undermines the vital *Body Before Skill* concept and gives athletes a false sense of achievement when they "hit."

REALITY B challenges

- Promotes a fixed mindset which can lead to a sense of failure, potential mental blocks while demolishing the sense of accomplishment of the entire season.

- One routine should not define the journey, and it should certainly not determine the success or failure of an athlete's progress.

Are we saying that "hitting zero" should not be the goal or the standard? Surely if we want cheerleading to be seen as a serious, possibly even an Olympic sport - shouldn't we be striving for hitting zero across the board? Before we answer this question, let's look at other sports and industries and the expectations they set.

Professional Sport - you may have seen the film *Moneyball*. The theme revolves around the idea that performance statistics were not necessarily a deciding factor when choosing players. For decades, baseball (and many other sports) athletes were not selected through their statistics, but rather a mix of 'star quality' and what scouts thought of their overall performance. The Oakland Athletics, using mathematical statistics, turned an entire industry around by putting together a team of misfits that coincidentally had the highest success rates in baseball. These rates were nowhere near 100%, but rather hovered around the 50-60% mark. In baseball, 50-60% is what was considered excellent.

In professional sports, we tend to also speak of losses and wins not just as a consequence of the winning team's extraordinary performance, but often as a consequence of the losing team being below par.

Olympic Sports - Qualifying for an Olympic sport is a whole other ordeal. The Olympics selection committee doesn't necessarily care about how an athlete looks on the cover of a magazine: the selection process is much more mathematical. Even though the overall execution is exceptionally high there is still a margin of error - otherwise, we would not have enough range for reasonable rankings. Think of ice-skating, gymnastics, diving - or all other sports scored by judging: yes, perfection is the holy grail and when it's achieved it's a wonderful thing. Athletes receive standing ovations and admiration for life.

Going back to cheer, we need to look at our scoring system overall and what it's saying to our athletes and our coaches. Is the "hitting zero" stamp useful, or is it hindering our perception of success? Is expecting perfection the most effective way to push high levels of execution, or is it reinforcing a sense of failure when 100% does not happen, pushing our sport further towards a fixed mindset standard?

Reality A makes failure an assumption and disregards true athletic development, falling into the pitfall of "let's hope the others do worse so we can win".

Reality B makes the fear of making a mistake define who we are and engulf us to the point where we become more terrified of making a mistake than we are excited about obtaining gold.

The rare, holy grail of realities: "C" is an outlook where overall execution trumps a margin of mistake. Where 'hitting zero' is neither a miracle nor an expectation, but a triumph. Where our athletes and coaches can define success by their journey, not just by their destination. When, sometimes, a second place can feel just like first.

A WINNING ATTITUDE

In this chapter about mind and focus, we've explored the many ways in which we can prevent psychological pitfalls for our athletes and build strong mental toughness. Again, we have just scraped the tip of the iceberg, and I highly recommend further reading. *UnBlocked: The Walls Come Tumbling Down* is by Jeff Benson, an esteemed colleague and a dear friend. He has been of great assistance to me in compiling this chapter of *Body Before Skill*.

I want to close this section by speaking about the winning attitude our athletes can achieve by mastering total fitness. How do we prepare ourselves and our athletes for greatness, after we have discovered that expecting perfection can cause the damaging effects of a fixed mindset and all that follows? First, it's time for a little backstory.

As I have focused my coaching career on helping other teams and developing programmes that can be widespread, I have personally gone down a cheer career that is quite uncommon in our industry. I chose not to focus my energies on growing my own cheer programme, opting instead to have a very small team in London merely as a creative outlet (and testing field for my theories and fitness programmes).

There is one peculiarity about the team I coach: the primary goal of Zoo is not competitive. In short, 'Zoo' (which is what then inspired the nickname that became my identity) represented an eclectic group of cheerleaders from different teams in the UK. It so happened that when the concept was born, most of these cheerleaders belonged to a team which had a name associated to an animal (Panthers, Tomcats, Foxes, etc…) - hence why as a collective, we were a 'Zoo'. These cheerleaders still competed with their own teams, but wanted to come together and expand their horizons by earning money to fund their dance and cheer hobbies through paid work ranging from TV show appearances, to product launches, movie premieres (my personal favourite being our photo shoot with Channing Tatum) and a number of PR events.

We decided to add competitive teams as we attracted a number of dancers with little cheer experience. I've always wanted to ensure that anyone joining Zoo gets competition experience so that they could be at the top of their game for professional work. My aim was never to develop a Worlds team with Zoo; it was to use this experience to 'bootcamp' our rookies into having a solid technique as well as a means to sell the team truly as the top professional cheerleaders in the UK. As we were focused on dance, we concentrated mainly on Senior Open Pom. (In future, and as my work commitments outside of London develop and I focus on more work at a more international level through Cheerobics®, Zoo members will continue to compete in their own time but we may not compete as a team.)

You might be wondering what this has to do with a winning attitude. How can an all star team or gym possibly relate to such a different type of cheerleading? Because of the way in which these teams performed at competitions was nothing short of miraculous; and regardless of the context, I truly believe the lessons can be used for any competitive cheerleading scenario. Why miraculous? The teams I have brought to competitions since 2012 have consisted of up of 90% rookies - most of which have never even cheered before in their lives, let alone competed. And guess what? Our 2016 team which had only been together for six months won gold at FC regionals and silver at BCA Nationals - 1.5 points behind a worlds team. Even more insane? Our 2014 team won Dance Grand Champions at BCA Nationals - we put the team together just four months prior with complete newbies to cheerleading.

Even with the greatest potential of each individual athlete, and the transferrable skills from dance, how is it possible that a team who had only been together for three months and trained for less than 40 hours in total win Grand Champions in a discipline that they had never trained in before? Does this not go against the deliberate practice/progression guidelines we just discussed? No, because all did was play the cards we were dealt with to the best of our abilities.

I am not saying this is a blueprint that will guarantee success, but when I applied the method below, I generally achieved a high rate of success. This included:

1. Choreographing to the athlete's ability and strengths.

2. Studying the event provider scoresheet and style.

3. Setting out a clear strategy for the division, without over-promising.

4. Setting precise expectations and scoresheet goals for the team.

5. Drilling execution like there was no tomorrow.

6. Conditioning the team through effective periodisation and progressive overload.

7. Focusing on team bonding through shared experiences.

8. Being adaptable and reactive when we hit hurdles.

9. Strong use of visualisation and Worlds videos.

10. Developing a winning attitude.

The most important part was to take the team through points 1-9 to get to the last point: the winning attitude. By doing this, the confidence I was able to instate in our athletes was not through words, but based on facts - even though we were up against the impossible. To the athletes, the points above translated to:

1. You have been given a routine that highlights your strengths; you have nothing to hide behind.

2. The routine has been designed to give you the best chance at scoring as highly as possible at this competition.

3. You know who we're competing against, and these are their strengths and weaknesses.

4. This is where you stand in the different score categories; this is what you need, and here is how we're going to get there.

5. When you step onto the mat, you will have drilled these skills to the best of your ability so that it will be embedded in your muscle memory.

6. You are working to gradually train your endurance and execution so that by the time you're on the mat, there will be no surprises and you can perform to the best of your ability.

7. You are a team who loves to hang out together as a unit; there are no cliques. There is only the spirit that bonds you together and the personality you have developed as a group.

8. You know how to deal with last-minute situations without being flustered. Anything can happen. The show must go on.

9. You know what the best in the world look like when they perform. Regardless of your skill level, you too can perform like them by embodying your favourite athlete. Even if you're not a Worlds athlete you can certainly act and perform like one on stage.

10. Because of the points above, you have all the reasons and tools to know you can reach for our goal. Go out there and get those points you have worked so hard for.

I have also found that working towards a scoresheet has been a more effective way to get a good placement, as opposed to focusing the team on the placement itself. Not only does it makes the goals more tangible, it also reduces the chances of inducing a fixed mindset. The chances of placing top three may be slim, so pushing for the top range for individual scores can be more realistic and provides an excellent fallback/learning point. "Oh no we came 5th" translates to "Wow, we got some great scores on X, Y, Z and we need some more work on A and B." It then provides a good focus for the team in contrast to a generic statement like "we need to be better to be successful." Furthermore, this fosters good sportsmanship. In a sport based on judging rather than opposition, instead of an "us versus them" attitude, it becomes "how can we get better with every competition." Growth. Mindset.

Of course, every coach will have their preferred method. I have found that this way provides a fun atmosphere for the team and creates less pressure without losing focus. Here are a few concepts that are useful as you approach the day of competition:

Banning Doubt: If you run two computer programs simultaneously, one called "I can" and the other "I might fail." The computer's RAM will be split between "I can" and "I might fail" and therefore, there is a 50/50 chance that one will be the outcome. This is a white horse versus a black horse. Explain this analogy to athletes so they understand that especially at competition, 100% of their energy and focus needs to be on the best possible outcome.

Walk in like you've already won: There is one thing that distinguishes Team USA at the Olympics from every other country. They walk in with style and swagger like they have already won. Winning is an attitude, and it has nothing to do with arrogance. Your attitude has nothing to do with how you feel about other teams because this fosters self-doubt and negativity. It's about getting to competition day knowing YOU are the best YOU can be, and you can't wait to show it off.

Butterflies into fire: Using the 1st law of Thermodynamics, you know that energy cannot be created or extinguished, but it can be transformed. Asking athletes to get rid of their nerves is like asking the ocean to stop moving. It's not going to happen. Instead, use different methods to help your athletes to turn their 'butterflies' (nerves) into 'fire' (hype). Remembering that everyone will have their preferred method: some will do this by internalising their focus (such as mental rehearsal and thinking logically) while others will prefer to externalise it (dancing, chanting, singing, etc). Consider group pep talks but also do this in smaller groups when needed.

Showing off: The time to show off what you've got is NOW. Everything an athlete has been working towards boils down to now: Skills have been learned, routine has been drilled, and you may have had a few last-minute dramas (it wouldn't be cheer without a bit of drama anyway). These are the cards you have been dealt with and it's time to make the best out of it, not to make excuses. Each athlete needs to step onto the mat with pride, delivering a performance that they will be proud of. It's your time to shine. It's time to show off.

3 focus words: Pep talks or prayers before stepping onto the mat can make or break what the team is about to do. Just like in a good fable, your pep talk needs to have a moral at the end. This conclusion needs to be what the athletes will be thinking about as they perform. Every team, every competition will be different. It can be performance energy, more technical, or spiritual. Whatever your focus is, boil it down to three distinct words and create your pep talk around them. This way, you can finish strong with these three words, and you can rest assured that your athletes will narrow their focus instead of having their minds swarming with a million other thoughts.

Regardless of the coaching style you prefer, these are tricks that have served me well in creating a winning attitude, even when faced with an adverse situation. The worst outcome I have encountered by using these methods is that my athletes did their absolute best and had a great time. And who can complain about that?

4

CHEERLEADING AND THE HUMAN BODY

One of the biggest challenges that the coaching community faces is the relevance of sports science, essential fitness knowledge and how they can be a applied to cheerleading. Sure, books on sports science, sports performance and biomechanics have been available for a long time, but one of the biggest struggles that I had found when reading them (and when discussing these with other coaches) was *relevance to what we do*. All this science talk is very interesting and yes, "I now know the difference between aerobic and anaerobic respiration, yay me!" is all very well, but then what purpose does this all serve if I can't win more trophies or just get my team to perform better? This thought process is perfectly understandable because the connection between the two might seem so far-fetched that it can be perceived as irrelevant.

We can say the same thing about large advertising billboards (you better be ready for analogies, this section has TONS of them). If you look very closely at a large ad billboard you can't make much sense of it because you can only see random dots of colours blotches. They look like they make no sense whatsoever, yet all these pixels are connected to form part of a big picture and as soon as you step back, the image comes into focus as if by magic. This is the same as each individual element of the human body and how we can sharpen it to make the 'bigger picture' work better. We are, after all, complex biological machines and cheerleading is a series of biological sequences that our body needs to perform. In this chapter, I've attempted to break down these elements and connect them to how they can be applied to the sport we love so that it makes more sense to us. In the spirit of varied learning methods, if you find sections that just don't seem to skink in by reading, I highly encourage you to go on Youtube or Wikipedia and search the term that confuses you instead of just skipping over them.

There are tons of great free videos and animations online that can help illustrate these concepts. If you have joined one of the INTENSITY™ coach groups on Facebook, you can always ask questions and clarifications and our coaches will be happy to help you. Regardless: be curious, dig deeper, and watch yourself become a master puppeteer of cheer performance.

ENERGY & RESPIRATION

The body requires energy to carry out all its functions, anything from exercise to growth to digestion. Different food types are made up of various molecules, which are used for energy production and other functions such as insulation, growth and repair. For energy to be produced, food molecules need to be broken down and used efficiently.

Because fat is a more efficient way of storing energy (fat has more calories per gram than protein for example) all excess food is turned into fat and stored in the adipose layer under the skin. The rate at which cells are able to release energy from food or fat stores is known as the **metabolic rate**.

Fibre, which mainly consists of cellulose, cannot be broken down by the human digestive system. The roughage is therefore passed along the digestive system, aiding the passage of other waste products along the way, until it is excreted.

Food Type	Molecule	Stored molecule	Stored In	Primary Use	Kcal/g
Carbohydrate	Glucose	Glycogen, excess fat	Muscles, bones	Fuel	4
Fat	Fatty Acids	Fat	Adipose tissue	Fuel stores	9
Protein	Amino Acids	Excess as fat	Not stored in humans	Growth & Repair	4
Fibre	Cellulose	Excreted	Not stored	Aids digestion	2

Energy Production

Energy is produced when food molecules and stored fat molecules are broken down, releasing a molecule called ATP (adenosine *tri*phosphate). ATP is the energy molecule (the battery, if you will) that is used to fire up all functions of the body. ATP is not the energy itself, but a molecule that needs to be broken down in order to release the energy. When broken down, the molecule becomes *ADP* (adenosine *di*phosphate), and this transformation is what releases the energy.

	System	Uses	Oxygen	Production	Sports Example	Use
Anaerobic Respiration	Alactic	Stored ATP	Not Present	Very fast	Golf, long jump, one stunt, tumble	1-10 seconds
	Lactic	Glycogen	Not Present	Fast	Sprinting, initial part of a full-out cheer routine	20-90 seconds
Aerobic Respiration	Aerobic	Glycogen Fatty Acids	Present	Slow	Jogging, cycling, aerobics	1-2 hours

There are 3 energy systems that allow the creation and break-down of ATP to release energy.

- **Alactic:** First to fire up, uses quick, available sources of ATP, but only lasts up to 10 seconds. It's our body's ability to move quickly as a reflex from danger.
- **Lactic:** Takes a few seconds to kick in and can be sustained for up to 90 seconds unassisted, giving the body time to kick-start the aerobic system. This system kicks in again when the aerobic system is at full capacity (usually after the body has reached 80% of its heart rate, or after a few hours of continuous exercise).

> ▸ **Aerobic:** The second system to kick in, starting at about 90 seconds or so, to take over from lactic respiration. It is a much more efficient and sustainable system to provide energy, and needs oxygen to work with glycogen from carbohydrates or fat from stores to create ATP. However energy is produced from breaking down fat stores instead of from food, so the muscles slow down by 20-30%. The system can last on its own under 80% maximum heart rate, for a few hours of continuous exercise.

During exercise, energy will be released by all three systems in different ratios. We store ATP in limited amounts, meaning that cells can work without the presence of oxygen (anaerobically) for a very short amount of time through existing ATP stores. This is achieved through the alactic (creatine phosphate) system, and only lasts for approximately the first 10 seconds of activity.

After the ATP stores have been used up, *ADP* (adenosine *di*phosphate) needs to be re-synthesised into ATP. This is where lactic acid respiration comes into place, which can re-synthesise ATP without the presence of oxygen. This system produces lactic acid as a byproduct, which is difficult to break down and is the reason we get a burning sensation in our muscles after hours of heavy exercise.

Because anaerobic respiration happens quickly, it allows the body to react fast, thus allowing us to avoid danger but also for more mundane tasks like dashing for the bus and rushing through the sliding doors. Sports such as golf, the long jump or sprinting, which require shorter times of activity at different intervals, are performed mainly through anaerobic respiration. In cheerleading, we use this for a tumble pass or to practice a stunt sequence or pyramid.

We then move on to using aerobic respiration to help our ATP resources which can work for a few hours as long as we don't over-exert ourselves. This system can produce an unlimited amount of ATP, but it is slow to engage and only works if the type of exercise is at a consistent and comfortable pace. Think of this system as a steam engine: slow to get started, consistent and reliable as long as you don't ask it to go too fast.

When the intensity of the exercise needs a boost or you increase the length of time (beyond an hour or two), the body will reach a threshold where there is not enough oxygen available to keep up with the demands of ATP production. The body initially responds by increasing oxygen intake by breathing in more air and then needs to kick in some boost from the lactic anaerobic respiration. The problem with this system is that it requires glycogen to create enough ATP and the body needs to take this from the muscles. This is one reason why marathon runners generally look much skinnier than other athletes; they rely mostly on anaerobic respiration to get them through the race as their muscles release their glycogen stores and literally 'waste' away.

HOW IS THIS USEFUL IN CHEERLEADING?

In some of the chapters in this book, we will discuss the different energy systems required during a full out routine, a training session and over a competition weekend. Understanding that there are distinctive energy systems that intertwine and piggyback off each other is a great way to train athletes to make the most out of their energy sources and get them performing at their peak. It will help you to make the call of whether you want to train many repetitions of a skill, or whether it's best to rest or alternate.

The science in the previous few pages may not necessarily be everyone's cup of tea. For those that, like me, prefer to picture things in their head: Are you ready for the **glow sticks analogy**?

Imagine your energy source comes in the form of glow sticks. The energy is stored in there, but to release it you need to break it. This is essentially how ATP molecules are. ATP is not the energy itself; the energy is *released* when the molecule breaks. Stores of ATP (our glow sticks) can either be made from fat (stored) or glycogen (bloodstream or muscles).

Let's say we're taking a hike in the woods and we encounter a bear (not a friendly one, sadly, this is bear wants to eat us). We sprint off like lightening. To do this, we need energy quick, so we can just use the glow sticks we carry around in our pocket. They're easily accessible and they will get us going pretty quickly. This is *alactic anaerobic respiration*. Since we can't carry around excessive amounts of glow sticks in our pockets, it will only help for the first 10 seconds. If the bear keeps chasing us through the hills we will probably need to look for more glow sticks in our backpack, which can get us going for another 90 seconds or so. To kick off our systems, our bodies need to rely on energy released WITHOUT oxygen because aerobic respiration (which requires oxygen) takes a while to kick in. This is *lactic anaerobic respiration*.

We're still running through the forest. The bear is still behind us. Luckily, we run past a shed where there are stores of glow stick boxes (handy!); we can run for another few hours at a steady pace. This is aerobic respiration, our main source of energy that will keep us going for a few hours (depending how fit we are).

Sadly, this bear is not giving up (thankfully even though he is stubborn, he's not fast enough to catch up with us). So our jog through the forest continues and we're running out of glow sticks to crack. We need more, but where do we get them from? We're going to have to barter with the black market. The currency? Muscle fibres. We can get enough glow sticks to last us all day, but we have to trade away our muscles because anaerobic respiration is kicking back in with a vengeance. This time it's not free: we need to pay the price.

In a cheerleading routine, energy systems don't stop and start. They support each other when they need it. The point at which they come in and how long the system is sustainable will differ from person to person. The best part, is that this can be trained through cardiovascular fitness.

THE CARDIOVASCULAR SYSTEM

The cardiovascular system is composed of the heart, blood and blood vessels. The function of the system is to pump the blood around the body in order to transport oxygen to all cells in the body while removing carbon dioxide and other waste products.

THE HEART

The heart is a double pump, activated by involuntary contractions of the cardiac muscles. It simultaneously pumps deoxygenated blood to the lungs and oxygenated blood to the rest of the body. The heart has four chambers surrounded by the cardiac muscles: two atriums, where the blood is received, and two ventricles, from which the blood is pumped out. The right side of the heart receives/pumps deoxygenated blood and the left side oxygenated blood.

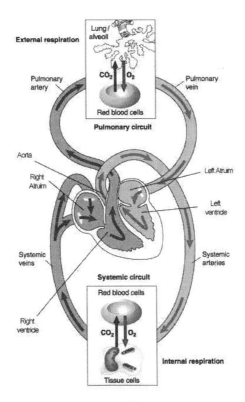

The heart receives deoxygenated blood in the right atrium, and pumps it to the lungs from the right ventricle through the pulmonary artery. Here, waste products (e.g. CO_2) are deposited and the blood receives oxygen through the capillaries. This then returns to the heart through the left atrium via the pulmonary vein, to be pumped to the rest of the body from the left ventricle and to the vena cava. This is called the circulatory system, which is shown in the diagram below.

The heart beats in two contractions: **systole** (blood is pumped out) and **diastole** (blood flows in). The rate of these contractions (heart rate) in a resting adult should be between 60 and 80 beats per minute. This increases with age.

The amount of blood pumped out per beat is known as the **stroke volume**. This is usually between 70-80ml per beat, but can increase if the individual is in excellent cardiac health. The **cardiac output** signifies the total amount of blood pumped out per minute, and can be calculated by multiplying the heart rate by the stroke volume.

HEART RATE x STROKE VOLUME = CARDIAC OUTPUT

VO2max measures the maximum amount of oxygen that the body can use. It is measured in millilitres per kilogram of body weight per minute (ml/kg/min). Training to increase VO2max is one of the most effective ways to develop endurance and overall sports ability.

BLOOD VESSELS

Blood consists of plasma (fluid), red blood cells, protective white blood cells, and platelets (responsible for repair). Red blood cells contain a red-pigmented protein called haemoglobin which carries oxygen throughout the body. The blood vessels transport a number of substances around the body. These include:

- Oxygen
- Nutrients
- Hormones
- Carbon Dioxide
- Heat
- Waste products from cellular respiration
- White blood cells

There are five main types of blood vessels in the body: veins, venules, capillaries, arterioles and arteries. Arteries carry blood away from the heart, veins carry blood towards the heart, and capillaries are present in the tissues, allowing diffusion and exchange of substances. The table illustrates the differences between veins and arteries. Capillaries are very small (only one cell thick!) which makes them very delicate, but risk of rupturing is not a health hazard. Nosebleeds and bruising are examples of damaged capillaries.

	Veins	**Arteries**
Blood	Carry deoxygenated blood (except for the pulmonary vein)	Carry oxygenated blood(except for the pulmonary artery)
Vessel wall	Thinner, less muscle	Thick, muscular
Direction	Transports blood towards the heart	Transports blood away from the heart
Pressure	Lower pressure	Higher pressure
Girth of cavity	Large	Narrow
Valves	Present to prevent backflow	Not present

HOW IS THIS USEFUL IN CHEERLEADING?

Understanding how blood transports oxygen around the body, is useful because it opens up the concept of trainability. By increasing VO2max, we *can* improve an athlete's ability to utilise oxygen because our bodies adapt by making the system more efficient: more red blood cells, more haemoglobin, more capillaries. Think about it like a delivery and pickup system where the lungs are the depot, the blood cells are the trucks, and haemoglobin are the boys carrying around the merchandise (oxygen) and picking up the trash (carbon dioxide). Wouldn't it be more efficient if the delivery system had more trucks, more boxes and a better road network (capillaries)?

Stamina is not just about how long it takes before an athlete runs out of breath; it's about *how much oxygen they can get to the muscles* so that they can perform better, last longer and be more stable. Training the cardiovascular system so that it's more efficient is giving the gift of resilience to athletes.

THE RESPIRATORY SYSTEM

Breathing is needed to supply oxygen to the body and rid it of carbon dioxide. It consists of three phases:

- **Inhalation:** air is breathed into the body
- **Exhalation:** air is breathed out
- **Gaseous exchange:** oxygen is taken in and carbon dioxide is removed

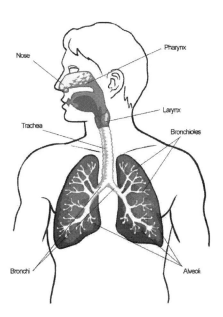

This process happens between 12 and 20 times per minute in the average adult, and is necessary for all organs and functions in the human body. Without it, cellular respiration cannot take place and cells, tissues, and organs would not be able to carry out their functions.

Ideally, air is inhaled through the nose as opposed to the mouth, because the nasal cavity makes the air warmer and damper, facilitating the assimilation of oxygen into the body. Air then passes into the larynx, through the **trachea**, **bronchi**, **bronchioles** and finally the air sacs known as the **alveoli**.

The alveoli are small, thin sacs which inflate and deflate with every breath, allowing oxygen to pass through into the bloodstream and let carbon dioxide out. **Diffusion** is the movement of molecules from an area of high concentration to an area of low concentration. Therefore, oxygen (which is highly concentrated in air) moves to the blood stream which has a low concentration. Carbon dioxide, which is highly concentrated in the venular bloodstream, is removed with exhaled air.

The vast number of the small, thin alveoli means that collectively they have a high surface area. The higher the surface area, the greater capacity to facilitate diffusion. The alveoli are lined with a thick network of capillaries flowing with plenty of deoxygenated and oxygenated blood, necessary for gaseous exchange. As air is inhaled, the volume of the lungs increases. The total amount of air which the lungs can hold is known as the **lung capacity** which is measured in litres (usually about 6 litres in the average adult but lower in smokers and higher in athletes).

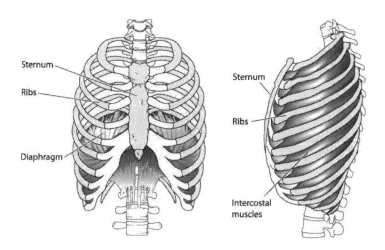

Once oxygen has been assimilated into the bloodstream and carbon dioxide released into the alveoli, air is exhaled out through the bronchioles, bronchi, trachea, larynx and finally the mouth. This entire process is controlled by the contraction and relaxation of the **diaphragm**: a flat, dome-shaped muscle found below the lungs which acts as a suction pump, working in conjunction with the intercostal muscles located between the ribs. When the diaphragm relaxes, the lungs enlarge and the alveoli expand, creating a depression which forces air in. When the diaphragm contracts, the alveoli deflate forcing air out.

HOW IS THIS USEFUL IN CHEERLEADING?

Breath control will help to reduce the average amount of breaths and will have a direct impact on the efficiency of the cardiovascular system. Training to reduce the breaths required during a full out will make an athlete's body more efficient in utilising oxygen and will also improve their total body stability. Good breath control helps us to focus and control our diaphragm, which has a direct impact on our core muscles, making us more in touch with our centre of gravity and thus, more stable.

THE SKELETON

When referring to the visible parts of the human body, the correct terms for these are **superior** (towards the head), **inferior** (towards the feet), **posterior** (back), **anterior** (front), **lateral** (side), **medial** (centre), **proximal** (closer) and **distal** (further).

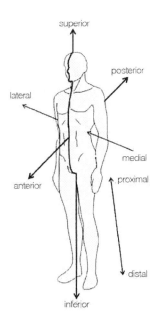

Bones & The Skeleton

The adult human skeleton is made up of 206 bones. It is necessary to give the body shape and support, allow movement, protect the muscles, store minerals, and for the production of white and red blood cells in the bone marrow. The skeleton can be divided into 2 parts:

> ‣ **The Axial Skeleton:** composed of the spinal structure, hips and head

> ‣ **The Appendicular Skeleton:** composed of the arms and legs

The cartilage found in between and around the bones prevents them from rubbing together and provides shock absorption. The process of cartilage turning into bone through time (as more minerals are stored and packed together) is called ossification. This bone growth starts in the 7th week of gestation and continues approximately until 25 years of age.

The degeneration of the bones (e.g. becoming thinner and more fragile) is known as osteoporosis. This is often caused by age and low oestrogen levels, but some types of this condition can also be genetically inherited. The body's 206 bones can be categorised into 4 shapes:

- **Long bones:** length is greater than the width (e.g. tibia)
- **Short bones:** length and width are almost equal (e.g. tarsals and carpals)
- **Flat bones:** thin compared to length and width of the bone (e.g. scapula)
- **Irregular bones:** irregular and complex shapes (e.g. vertebrae)

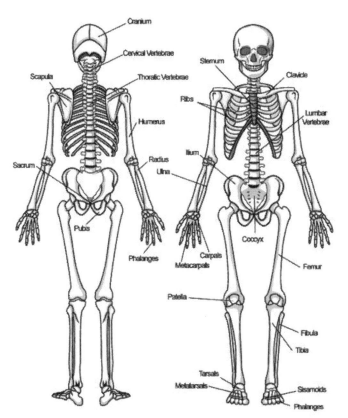

THE NECK & SPINE

The vertebral column is composed of 33 bones (vertebrae). These are subdivided into 4 groups, listed in the table below in descending order. The spine consists of 3 types of elements:

▸ **Single vertebral bodies:** Irregular bones which are placed one on top of the other to form the vertebral column. Each of the bones has a hole in the centre and they are stacked to form a tube that protects the spinal cord.

▸ **Spinal cord:** Long, thin, tubular central nervous tissue which, together with the brain, makes up the central nervous system.

▸ **Intervertebral discs:** Flat cushions with a jelly-like centre which prevents friction between the bones and protects from forceful shock or impact.

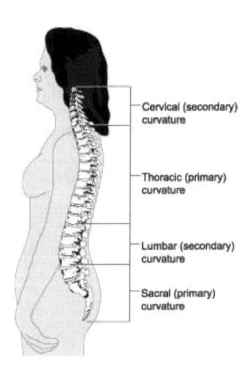

Cervical (secondary) curvature

Thoracic (primary) curvature

Lumbar (secondary) curvature

Sacral (primary) curvature

The majority of the spine's range of movement occurs in the upper thoracic region and the neck (cervical region). Movement in the lumbar and sacral region is much more limited with only 12-13% mobility. The spine's movement is possible through the stacking of the vertebrae, which create an interlocking joint system. The erector spinae is the main muscle group that gives the spine movement, with the sternocleidomastoid (SCM), trapezius and scalene muscles giving movement to the head. The top cervical vertebrae (the atlas) is shaped to fit in with the base of the head, while the second vertebrae (the axis) has a rod-like shaped point which shoots to the top of the spine allowing the head multi-directional movement.

The spine gets reinforcement through a network of tendons, ligaments and joint capsules, with the synovial fluid acting as lubrication to the vertebrae. The spine is critical not only to give our body structure, but also to form a protective fortress for our spinal cord which is the nerve transmitter between the brain and the rest of our body.

In its healthy state, the spine is straight from the back front and slightly s-shaped when looking from the side. However, over time there are a number of abnormal curvatures which can develop in the spine. These can be brought on by a number of factors including:

- **Daily life:** Wearing heels, slouching at desk, carrying heavy loads and bags on the shoulders unevenly, posture.
- **Emotional state:** Depressive states can cause slouching.
- **Nutrition:** Nutrient deficiencies including Vitamin D and calcium can lead to weak and malformed bone structures.
- **Pregnancy:** Weight of the womb will cause arching forward.
- **Sports:** Can cause the back to be curved in excess.
- **Hereditary factors:** Scoliosis and arthritis can be passed on through the genes.
- **Injuries:** To the feet, legs, hips, spine, or because of an adjusted posture.
- **Age:** Can lead to osteoporosis and development of bad posture.

HOW IS THIS USEFUL IN CHEERLEADING?

Athletes who complain about having a 'bad back' usually refer to problems in the lumbar spine (lower back). This is because it is the area where the majority of movement and weight bearing takes place. It requires a lot of flexibility especially in cheerleading. Flexibility, however, needs to be counteracted with strength - not just of the muscles, but of the connective tissue (tendons and ligaments). Remembering that we have 70% mobility in a healthy upper back and that it is used in every skill within cheerleading should prompt us to include more thoracic exercises on a daily basis. The reality is that most athlete's thoracic mobility is not as good as it should be. They overcompensate by using the lower back or shoulders which end up taking the impact, even though that's not what they are designed to do. Understanding the delicate balance of the spine and how it affects the rest of our body should prompt us to train shoulder and thoracic mobility much more frequently.

Within cheerleading, we are also told that the most important thing to protect when catching the flyer is the head. The head and the spine, if injured, is not just a question of pulling out of competition and wearing a cast. Because of the spinal cord, it's a question of life or death: injuries to this area can shut down a part the body or the entire body.

In my first few years of cheerleading, I witnessed an incident that scarred me for the rest of my life and put me in the direction of *'Body Before Skill'* as a mantra. The team I was on decided to try a new stunt. The team was ungoverned. Cheerleading was still a bit of a 'wild west' at this point in the UK and self-taught teams did the best they could. *'Body Before Skill'* was light-years away from being an accepted concept at this stage. At this point, it was more like, "I saw this thing online, let's chuck it!". We need to remember that this is still the case in many places where cheerleading is very new, ungoverned or underdeveloped.

Even though this approach made me relatively uncomfortable, especially as my conservative views were not always welcome, most of our training sessions were run on the basis of "let's see what we can throw." *Conditioning* was a term we only used in the context of what happens after shampooing your hair. The term *progressions* was being used, but more in the context of describing someone's career than anything to do with building cheerleading skills.

So, we're at training and the stunt being 'chucked' was a partner stunt pendulum from extension: it twisted backwards so during the dismount, the flyer cradled facing the back and got caught by three bases while the partner stunt base held onto the feet. This time, the flyer fell through the catchers and her head smacked on the floor with a sound that will haunt me for the rest of my life. Thankfully, the flyer ended up being fine and there was no break, bleeding or internal injury. Clearly, she was a tough cookie, even though she was barely able to speak, recognise where she was, or who she was while we waited for the ambulance over the next 30 minutes. Witnessing this gave me a feeling that I will never shake off. I was there, knowing things did not look right, and I was not in a position to say "STOP. This isn't right".

I don't blame anyone for what happened; if anything I blame myself for not speaking up when my gut feeling was shouting inside me. It was a lack of education at the time when cheerleading was still relatively in the 'dark ages' for us. However, I knew that this should have never been allowed to happen and that this was not going to be the first or the last time such an incident would happen in cheerleading. A flyer across the world might have had the same incident with a less resilient bone structure or absorbent connective tissue - and could have died.

I'm not in the business of scaremongering: I just want to bring attention to one part of our body where neglect can be catastrophic. If you understand the basics of how the spine works, its role in keeping us alive and functioning - you will understand that we need to protect it, understand its limitations and make it as resilient as we can. Cheerleading is a risk, but each risk needs to be calculated, especially when it comes to the spine and the neck. A stunt is not worth a life.

MUSCLE ANATOMY

Muscles are responsible for movement of the human body, both as a whole and for its organs and systems. Muscles are needed to:

- Produce movement
- Provide stability
- Move substances around the body
- Produce heat

There are three types of muscles:

- **Involuntary muscles:** These are smooth muscles that contract unconsciously. An example of these are the muscles that line the oesophagus which contract and relax, allowing us to swallow food without conscious thought.

- **Voluntary muscles:** These muscles are attached to the bones (skeletal muscles) and we are able to control them. Voluntary muscles are used during exercise and movement. All skeletal muscles are voluntary muscles.

- **Cardiac muscle:** These muscles are only found in the heart and contract/relax to pump blood around the body.

SKELETAL MUSCLES

There are approximately 650 skeletal muscles in the body which make up between 30% - 50% of total body weight. They are attached to the bone via a tendon or other connective tissues and always cross at least one joint. Muscles move in pairs, contracting, relaxing, and assisting the joint. The table in the next page uses a bicep curl as an example of how the different muscles work together to open and close the elbow joint. This is relevant to help us understand that it's not just about conditioning our bicep alone, for example, but the full network of muscles and the kinetic chain that creates the movement. We need to remember that athletic training should be aimed at functionality, not at aesthetics, and training all the muscles will make sure the resistance is equally distributed so that some muscles are not overworked.

Role	Definition	Muscle example (in bicep curl)
Prime mover	Main muscle performing the movement	Bicep
Antagonist	Muscle performing the opposite movement	Tricep
Fixator	Helps maintain the correct position	Rhomboids
Synergist	Assists the prime mover	Deltoid

When we say the term 'muscle' it's easy to think of a unit in isolation. Instead, we need to think of muscles as a group of smaller muscle fibres, connected together and merging into connective tissue. There is no real beginning and end between a muscle and a tendon, and the muscle itself is made up of packs of fibres that are wrapped tightly together by a film of fascia (primarily made of collagen), almost like a malleable cling film that packs together muscle fibres, units, organs and blood vessels.

MUSCLE NAMES

It's important to know the basic muscle groups so that we fully understand the kinetic chain of each movement and how the muscles work together. The inner core muscles (which will be discussed more in-depth in later chapters as they are of great importance in cheerleading) can be found underneath the rectus abdominis layer.

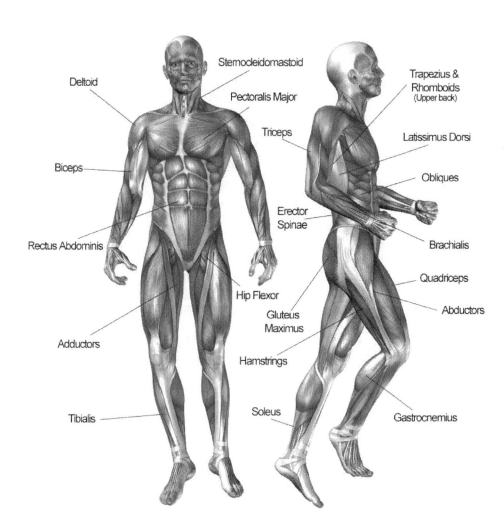

FIBRE TYPES & CONTRACTIONS

Muscles are also made up of two types of fibres:

▸ **Slow twitch:** Red in colour and are smaller, more compact. They contract slowly and are used for lower intensity, slow, aerobic exercise which requires effort over a period of time. People that have a higher proportion of slow twitch muscles tend to be better at endurance sports such as marathons. Cheerleaders with more slow-twitch muscles than fast-twitch tend to struggle with the speed required to achieve jumps or tumbling.

▸ **Fast twitch:** White in colour and bulkier. These contract twice as fast as slow twitch muscles and are used for high intensity and shorter bursts of exercise (think of the physique of a sprinter compared to a marathon runner).

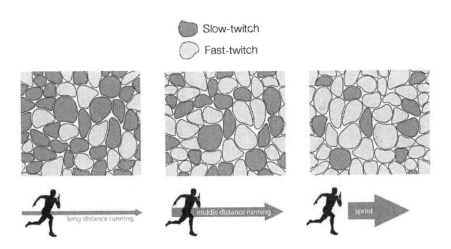

Different muscles have different proportions of each muscle fibre type depending on their main function and development. Normal humans tend to have a 50/50 distribution of these types but some people will genetically have more of one or the other. It's not the type of training that determines the ratio of fast-twitch or slow-twitch. Instead, an athlete will commonly decide to follow a sporting path that is more suited to their body type and performance. However, muscles can be trained and conditioned to increase speed, power and reaction time through **selective recruitment.** Muscles have the ability to contract in three different ways: isometrically, concentrically and eccentrically.

HOW IS THIS USEFUL IN CHEERLEADING?

Muscles are probably the first thing we think about when we think of conditioning. However, it is understanding *how* the muscles are structured, how they connect to the bones and blend with the connective tissue which will give us a better understanding of how we can train them. It's not about how big and defined they are; it's about understanding how we can make the most out of them and answer these questions:

- How can we grow them?
- How can we stretch them?
- How can we make them stronger?
- How can we make them go faster?
- How can we make them last longer?
- What is the most effective way to train for a specific function?
- What type of skills or training type is athlete X more suited to?
- How can we train athlete X to maximise his/her abilities?
- How can we explain a skill at a kinesiology level?
- What kind of contraction do we need to train?

Knowing how to answer the questions above is much more valuable than the answers themselves because it makes our possibilities become infinite.

JOINTS

Joints have two major functions:

- **Stability:** The ability to control the movement from an external force, using a combination of neuromuscular reflexes and the strength/elasticity of the connective tissues.

- **Mobility:** The ability to move the joint through its available range of motion before being restricted by muscles and connective tissues.

The 'holy grail' of a joint is to develop an equal balance between mobility and stability: strength versus movement. Both are important elements of training within cheerleading - stability needs to be trained before mobility to reduce the risk of injury (i.e. the joints would be too weak to sustain the movement). However, once an adequate amount of stability has been reached, the joint also requires enough mobility in order to maximise its range of motion and avoid injury due to movement limitations. Balance between the two is key, as well as an understanding of how each of our joints are utilised and endangered during cheerleading activities.

Bones are connected by the joints which are composed of:

- **Ligaments:** Connecting bone to bone.
- **Tendons:** Connecting muscles to bones.
- **Cartilage:** Specialised connective tissue lining the articulating surfaces of joints.
- **Bursae:** Fluid filled sacs to cushion the friction points between bones and other structures (i.e. tendons).
- **Synovium:** Also known as the synovial membrane, this is the tissue lining the joint capsule which is in direct contact with the synovial fluid.
- **Synovial Fluid:** Acts as a lubricant to reduce friction and facilitate movement.

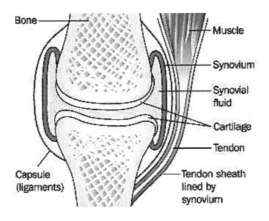

There are three types of joints in the human body:

▸ **Fibrous (fixed):** The bones are joined together and are unable to move (e.g. the skull).

▸ **Cartilaginous (movable):** The bones are tightly connected together and have some movement (e.g. the spine).

▸ **Synovial (freely movable):** The joints are the most used in an exercise context. These joints secrete synovial fluid from the synovial membrane to help lubricate the joints and facilitate mobility (e.g. the elbow).

A rapid hyperextension of the joints can cause injury in the form of a **strain** (to the tendons) or a **sprain** (to the ligaments). It is crucial that all joints are correctly warmed up, mobilised and stretched to their current range of motion before training. This ensures that the tissues and synovial fluid are warm enough for the demands of cheer which will also aid in avoiding injuries. At the same time, over-stretching the joint before skill training will reduce the explosiveness of the joint's movement, and potentially lead to an injury. The joint needs to be strong as well as flexible.

Terminology used to describe joint movement:

Movement	Return movement	Joints
Flexion: reducing the angle	**Extension:** increasing the angle	Knee, hip, shoulder, elbow, wrist, fingers, toes and spine.
Elevation: lifting or raising	**Depression:** dropping or lowering	Shoulders
Adduction: move towards the body (midline)	**Abduction:** bring away from the body (midline)	Hip, shoulder
Pronation: turning the medial side towards the ground	**Supination:** turning the medial side upwards	Wrist, ankle
Plantarflexion: pointing the toes down	**Dorsiflexion:** flexing toes up	Ankle
Protraction: rounding the shoulder forward	**Retraction:** pulling the shoulders back.	Shoulders
Rotation: pivoting around the long axis of the bone		Spine (cervical, thoracic, lumbar vertebrae)

TYPICAL JOINT ISSUES

Each joint can be exposed to variety of injuries and trauma. These injuries are classified as **acute**, **sub-acute** or **chronic**. With acute and sub-acute injuries, there is normally an accident or sudden force applied, resulting in the injury. With a chronic injury, there is normally no direct impact or force involved. It is usually due to repetitive motion with incorrect technique or posture that results in the injury. An athlete's genetics, nutrition and physical history will all have an impact on how their joints respond to and recover from injury.

The following list shows general issues which can be experienced by all joints of the body:

> ‣ **Tightness and stiffness:** Caused by constant use in daily life and cheer training, (DOMS) or delayed onset muscular soreness is part of the body's regenerative cycle. Regular stretching, mobility exercises and alternative training practices can help speed recovery.

> ‣ **Muscle inflammation:** Inflammation is part of the healing process in the body and is needed to help repair damage. However, excessive inflammation can cause pain and may be a sign of a chronic problem. Cryotherapy or the use of ice packs can help relieve both pain and inflammation.

> ‣ **Muscle strain, tear or rupture:** Microscopic, partial or complete tear caused when the muscle gets overstretched or exerted with excessive force beyond its elastic properties.

> ‣ **Muscle spasm:** Caused by tears and sprains. The body's natural defence mechanism is to lock the muscle, preventing further damage.

> ‣ **Sprain:** Caused by microscopic tears or over stretching the ligaments.

> ‣ **Tendinopathy:** Common term is tendinitis, which essentially means inflammation of the tendon. As discussed previously, inflammation is part of the body's healing process.

Three main points in which a tendon can be injured are the musculotendinous junction where the tendon connects to the muscle, the mid-tendon or non-insertional tendinopathy and finally the tendon insertion, where the tendon connects to the bone.

▸ **Dislocation:** Caused when the head of the bone slips out of its placement partially or fully, usually as a result of a traumatic force. First aid and expert medical advice should be sorted as soon as possible.

▸ **Bursitis:** When the bursae around the joints becomes inflamed due to overuse, trauma or systemic disease.

▸ **Fractures:** Splitting or fragmenting of a bone, generally after a fall or impact. There are also stress fractures which are normally the result of 'over training' or incorrect training and management.

▸ **Arthritis:** Two types being rheumatoid and osteoarthritis, resulting in the degeneration of the articular cartilage. Osteoarthritis is commonly referred to as overuse arthritis.

THE SHOULDER JOINT

The shoulder is a ball-and-socket joint that links the upper arm to the shoulder blades, and is made up of four separate joints. The humerus bone (upper arm) has a large rounded head that moves within a socket in the scapula (shoulder blade). It also includes the clavicle, which acts as a fixator to give the joint more stability. The joint is covered in articular cartilage to aid movement. The shoulder forms part of a kinetic chain that includes the skull, jaw, neck, back and arm. The muscles involved are the deltoids, biceps and rotator cuff, which consists of four muscles that link the shoulder blade to the humerus. The joint is strengthened through connective tissue known as the shoulder capsule and ligaments.

The specific issues linked to the shoulder include:

‣ **Tightness and stiffness:** Caused by the daily use of the shoulder, in cheer training, desk and computer-based occupations, overuse of handheld mobile devices, lifting and carrying in the frontal plane. It can be relieved by regular stretching to extend the shoulder ROM as well as exercises which strengthen the back to improve overall posture.

‣ **Tendinitis:** Caused by inflamed tendons due to excessive stress and repetition of similar movements: this is one of the most common shoulder complaints in cheerleading due to the shoulder's importance in many of our movements.

‣ **Rotator cuff injuries:** Due to repetitive stress to the major tendons which become inflamed and get pinched in the small space between the humerus and the scapula, when the arm is raised above shoulder height. If this is left untreated, it can lead to a rotator cuff tear.

‣ **Frozen shoulder:** Tightening of the shoulder capsule, caused either by overuse or underuse, where the shoulder to become immobilised, meaning limited ROM. Women tend to be more susceptible to this than men, especially during the older years.

‣ **Shoulder separation:** An impact at the tip of the shoulder can cause the joint between the clavicle and shoulder blade to sprain and swell, which may result in the dislocation or separation of the collarbone.

‣ **Dislocation:** Caused when the humerus bone slips partially out of the socket. It can be a one-off or repetitive condition that may require surgery.

‣ **Collarbone bruise:** Because the clavicle is so prominent, a trauma or impact can cause bruising of the soft tissue or the bone itself.

‣ **Fractures:** The humerus and the collarbone can fracture after a fall or impact.

THE HIP JOINT

The hip joint is the most stable joint of the body, but can get more fragile with inactivity and age rather than over-use (though this is also possible). It is a ball-and-socket joint made up of the three bones of the pelvis; the pubis, ischium, and ilium (hipbone) where the femur (bone in upper leg) is connected in a deep socket. The head of this bone is round and covered in cartilage, allowing it to move freely in a number of directions. The hamstrings, gluteus maximus, and deep core muscles (iliac and psoas) are responsible for keeping the hip joint stable. The joint gets reinforcement and stabilisation through tendons, ligaments and a joint capsule. Another major player in the hip joint is the iliotibial band (ITB), which runs laterally all the way down to the knee.

The hip forms the kinetic chain between the back and the legs, all the way down to the foot. The sciatic nerve, which starts in the spine, crosses down through the hip and then down to the legs to allow muscle contraction.

The specific issues linked to the hip include:

- **Dislocation:** Extremely uncommon but still possible with a large trauma. Can cause the bone to die and lose functionality unless it is attended to quickly.
- **Stress fractures:** Hairline fractures in the femur due to one-off or repetitive impact which can cause a mild pain. This often goes undetected which can cause a problem later on.
- **Fractures:** Although unlikely, the femur or pelvis can fracture after a fall or impact (such as a bad cradle of stunt fall to a hard surface or from a critical height).
- **Hip bone bruise:** As the ilium can be prominent, a trauma or impact can cause bruising of the soft tissue or the bone itself.

THE KNEE JOINT

The knee is the largest and most complex joint in the human body. It is known to be capable of explosive power and bears most of our weight, but at the same time is extremely delicate and is the joint most vulnerable to overuse injury and trauma.

It consists of the junction between the femur (thigh bone) and the tibia (shin). In between these bones there are two menisci: discs of cartilage which absorb impact. The kneecap (patella) is a circular bone disc that protects the knee joint, stabilised by tendons from the femur and tibia. The fibula is also connected to the joint by tendons and ligaments. The knee is part of the kinetic chain that includes the pelvis, hip, legs and ankles.

The hamstrings and quadriceps (in addition to smaller muscle groups, tendons, ligaments and the joint capsule) keep the joint stable and enable movement. The joint is covered in articular cartilage to aid movement. The most notorious ligaments of the knee joint are the collateral and cruciate ligaments (ACL and MCL) which cross over the knee and the ITB which secures the lateral movement of the knee.

The specific issues linked to the knee include:

> ‣ **Muscle inflammation:** Excessive stress and build-up of lactic acid commonly in the quadriceps, hamstrings and tibialis can cause chemical changes in the muscles, resulting in an inflammation.
>
> ‣ **Muscle sprain/ligament tear:** Caused by an over stretching of the ligaments or microscopic tears. ACL and MCL sprains and tears are the most common, especially with females past the age of puberty due to the increased angle outward from the knee to the hip. Landing on the feet whilst twisting upon impact is a major cause of ligament damage to the knee.
>
> ‣ **Jumper's knee:** A type of tendinitis where the tendons of the patella becomes inflamed due to excessive jumping and absorbing impact.

‣ **Tendinitis:** The tendons become inflamed due to excessive stress and repetition: this is one of the most common knee complaints found in cheerleading.

‣ **Meniscus tear:** The cartilage discs can get trapped and pinched between the two bones as a result of an intense impact. This can result in pain when walking and climbing stairs and may result in a knee lock.

‣ **Iliotibial band syndrome (ITBS):** The repeated rubbing of the tightened ITB against the knee edges, causing irritation to the outside of the knee.

‣ **Dislocation:** Caused when the patella partially or fully slips out of its placement, usually as a result of a traumatic blow.

‣ **Patella degeneration:** Wear and tear of the cartilage inside of the patella.

‣ **Fractures:** The top of the tibia and the patella can fracture after a fall or impact (most commonly during tumbling).

THE ANKLE & FOOT JOINT

The ankle is the connection between the highest bone of the foot, the talus, and the lower parts of the tibia and fibula. These two leg bones cup the talus, and the bones are covered in articular cartilage to aid movement. The foot itself is made up of 28 bones including tarsals, metatarsals, phalanges, calcaneus and sesamoids (at the base of the big toe). The bones are tightly packed in a close space, interconnected in a network of 32 joints. As a unit, they are stronger than the hand because it is designed to bear the majority of body weight.

The gastrocnemius, soleus, and tibialis are the muscles that provide movement as well as stability in combination with the achilles tendon, ligaments and joint capsules. The issues specific to the ankle and foot include:

‣ **Muscle inflammation:** More serious here than anywhere else in the body. If fluids get trapped in the foot it can solidify if not treated in time, causing long-term damage and inhibiting movement.

‣ **Shin splints:** A type of muscle strain that can result at the front of the ankle and the shin. This can be seen mostly in recreational, school or college cheer where cheerleading is practiced on hard surfaces. Extra absorbent footwear can be a good way to prevent this.

‣ **Muscle tear or rupture:** Very uncommon in the foot, but if this happens with the achilles tendon it will require surgery to repair.

‣ **Muscle sprain:** Caused by an over stretching of the ligaments or microscopic tears. Over stretching of the ligaments on the lateral side of the ankle is known as an inversion sprain and can be very common in cheerleading particularly due to pin/pop down dismounts and tumbling landings.

‣ **Tendinitis:** Tendons becoming inflamed due to excessive stress and repetition. This can be most commonly seen on the Achilles tendon. Allowing adequate warm up and stretching of the ankle and foot prior to more intense exercises will ensure the Achilles is pliable and flexible enough to withstand the demands of tumbling and jumps.

‣ **Nerve damage:** The nerves of the foot can become pinched, compressed or trapped between the bones of the foot and can cause burning sensations, pain, or numbness in different areas of the foot.

‣ **Dislocations:** Can happen as a result of a fall or bad landing.

‣ **Fractures:** Can be a result of a severe impact, and most commonly affects the lower parts of the heel bone (which can also be a result of a poorly absorbed landing).

‣ **Stress fractures:** Can emerge as a result of long-term, repeated impact on the sesamoid bones when landing on the balls of the foot. This is especially common with recreational and sideline cheerleading when performing and training on hard surfaces and with poor footwear. Wearing shoes with adequate support will help reduce the this.

▸ **Foot structure alterations:** (such as bunions, hammer toe, mallet toe or flat feet) Can be a result of genetics combined with overuse and poor footwear.

THE HAND & WRIST JOINT

The wrist is a collection of 8 bones (the carpals) connected to the radius and the ulna. The joints are covered in articular cartilage to aid movement. The hand is made up of 19 bones including the metacarpals and phalanges which are bound together by 14 joints. This allows the fingers to flex closely together and move independently, with the thumb carrying out opposable movement to the other fingers to facilitate grip and skilful manipulation. The joint gets reinforcement through the joint capsule, tendons and ligaments. The hand is unique in having plates of cartilage on the palm of the hands where the phalanges meet.

The issues linked to the hand and wrist include:

> ▸ **Muscle inflammation:** A huge issue for the wrist, but less common than the foot as it does not bear weight on a day-to-day basis so it has opportunity to heal. The build-up of lactic acid can cause chemical changes in the muscle, resulting in inflammation, and if fluids get trapped in the wrist and hand they may solidify if not rested or treated in time causing long-term damage. 'Sore wrists' are a common complaint of tumblers and bases and although seemingly unavoidable, can be relieved through wrist strengthening and mobilising exercises during warm-up.
>
> ▸ **Hand cramp:** A mild form of inflammation which is caused by constant gripping action (basing for example).

- **Jammed finger:** A muscle sprain that is usually caused by an impact or bad grip, often as a result of basing or tumbling. The finger may also become dislocated.

- **Tendinitis:** Tendons inflamed due to excessive stress and repetition of gripping, and usually affect the wrist and the thumb.

- **Fractures:** The base of the radius may become fractured as a result of a violent impact, but individual fingers may also suffer a break or fracture. Multiple fractures are also a possibility, even though this is relatively rare in cheerleading.

- **Nerve damage:** Nerves can become pinched, compressed or trapped between the bones of the hand and can cause burning sensations, pain, or numbness in different areas.

HOW IS THIS USEFUL IN CHEERLEADING?

Flexibility, stability and **mobility** are three fitness concepts that cause a great deal of confusion within cheerleading. We hear these three terms thrown around without necessarily understanding the distinction between them. Sprains and strains are equally responsible for the majority of injuries during cheerleading, but how can we apply the principles of conditioning to reduce the likelihood of these from occurring? We are told to stretch before training by some coaches, then we are told that stretching before training is bad for us. The confusion in when/how we should be stretching is one of the biggest contributors to joint injuries. Within our sport, we really need to make it a priority to understand joint integrity and how joints work with our body mechanics.

The information in this book has been designed to be accessible to anyone of any level who has an interest in sport. Getting to grips with this has another advantage: unlike the convoluted rule changes of our industry's divisions and age ranges, these facts don't change every year, even though our understanding will certainly evolve.

If you find yourself feeling confused about certain concepts, it might be tempting to skim over. But think this: what if that one paragraph you just skipped over could have saved the knee of one of your athletes the week before competition? It's perfectly fine to re-read, get up to grab a drink, and clear your minds. My favourite thing to do is look a video up online to help me visualise what couldn't get into my head by reading. After all, in the cheer world we're so used to Youtubing pyramids and stunts, why not start doing the same thing to help understand the inner workings of our bodies? It may not be as glamorous as watching the latest jaw-dropping stunt sequence, but a busted knee is far less appealing. Plus, consider that the athletes performing that same stunt can most probably perform the skill because they have solid joint integrity and years of conditioning that you can't see under the bodysuit of glitter.

5

TARGETED BODY TRAINING

In the previous chapter, we went through the different aspects of the human body and how each affects our performance. In *'Targeted Body Training'* we take these concepts and build on them by exploring the tools and techniques that are available to us to improve. The aim is to look at the individual parts of our bodies and apply your new tools directly to cheer skills and training. What can we do with ourselves? How will this impact individual skills? How do we fix existing issues? What guidelines and benchmarks can we give ourselves to make sure we're on the right track?

This section also includes ways to explain these concepts to athletes to help them understand, visualise and feel what good body control is like. Perhaps some athletes will take an interest in the theoretical aspects of *Body Before Skill* and perhaps some athletes will even read this book. Even though this is a curiosity that can be encouraged, it is not realistic to expect athletes of all ages to have such diligence in study. It is a coach's job not to overwhelm their athletes with fancy words but rather to translate this book into tangible guidance that the athletes can learn from.

POSTURE & STANCE

Very few people have a good posture and unfortunately, it's is one of the most common and preventable problems that limit a cheerleader's performance. In addition, an impact upon an incorrect postural alignment can cause injuries. Good posture will not only improve self-confidence and appearance, but it will also help the athlete's entire body be stronger, more efficient, and better when performing. To check if a posture is correct, the feet should not be more than two or four inches apart from each other and the spine should be in a natural S shape.

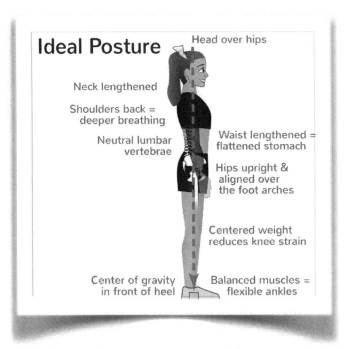

One step after good posture is a correct **athletic stance**. This position is a must for tumbling and jumps, and can also be found with small alterations in basing and flyer loads. It prepares the body for maximum explosion potential by concentric contraction of the hamstrings, lengthening the quadriceps for full **triple extension**. To achieve this position shoulders, knees and toes need to be in line with each other, with hips over heels, straight back, strong core and shoulders back.

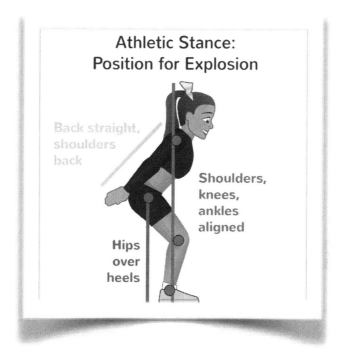

EXPLAINING POSTURE TO ATHLETES

‣ **Jumps:** Bad posture will limit the height of your jump. Imagine what happens if you're trying to compress and launch a spring. If the spring is slightly curved, it won't spring up as high. That's the same thing with your body and your spine.

‣ **Basing:** Good posture is CRUCIAL to bases. Bad posture during stunting can cause you to damage your back severely, lose control of your flyer (because the weight is not passing through the centre of gravity), and limit the power of your lift (because you are relying on your arms and legs alone to do the lifting).

‣ **Flying:** With good posture, you will have better balance and more control of your own body whilst it's in the air. It will help you develop the ability to perform more complex tricks and stretches.

> **Tumbling:** Tumbling greatly relies on the agility and flexibility of the spine. If you have poor posture to begin with, chances are that you will not have good enough foundations to perform your skills or you risk injuring yourself if you push yourself beyond your physical capability.

FIXING POSTURE ISSUES

Keeping an athletic posture is not as easy as asking cheerleaders to "keep your shoulders back." Maintaining good posture is a habit and it can be improved by strengthening different areas of the body.

> **Neutral posture awareness:** Finding a 'neutral posture' is a relaxing exercise that you can do when the team needs some downtime. This ensures athletes are aware of what is good or bad posture. If in a group, ask athletes to make a circle and face outwards so that they do not feel self-conscious. Pull the head up to lengthen the spine. Then tuck the tail out and under repeatedly and exaggeratedly until you the right point.

> **Strengthen upper back:** The main cause of a bad posture is a weak upper back (mainly the trapezius muscle). By doing exercises such as pushups and lateral pull-downs, athletes can strengthen these muscles which help keep shoulders back.

> **Increasing chest flexibility:** In combination with a weak back, chest muscles pull the shoulders in because they are get tight, so include a chest stretch in your cool-down.

> **Strengthen core:** With a weak core, athletes rely on their spine to hold their upper body upright. They need to develop a strong core to carry their body weight and relieve the spine.

> **Strengthen neck muscles:** We live in a society where we naturally strain our heads and neck forward to look at TV or computer screens. Also, shy individuals may look at their feet more, causing the spine to tilt. For good posture, remind athletes to stand strong, look up and keep their heads back.

CORE TRAINING

There is a specific set of muscles that is not covered in general muscle anatomy but are key when it comes to cheerleading. Ab muscles, which are trained for aesthetics, serve very little purpose in enhancing stability and strength required for tumbling, jumping or stunting.

On the other hand, the 'inner core' muscles are relatively unheard of within the cheer world but are a key component in yoga and pilates teachings. These muscles give the body stability and help to perform skills where the body requires the contraction of legs towards the chest (in jumps, tucks, pikes, etc). If trained appropriately and in isolation, they can perform wonders when it comes to the transformation of our athletes' skills. These are:

- ▸ **Transversus abdominis (TVA):** This is a layer of abdominal muscles that are found under the rectus abdominis (abs). This is THE most important ab muscle to be trained for strength and stability in sports, but is the most neglected one because it cannot be seen.

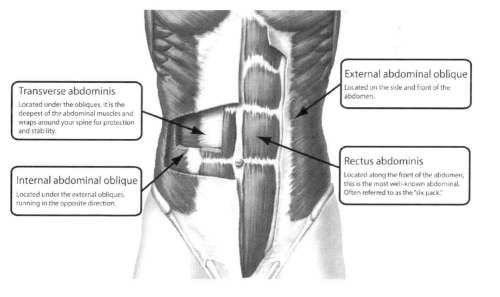

Transverse abdominis
Located under the obliques, it is the deepest of the abdominal muscles and wraps around your spine for protection and stability.

Internal abdominal oblique
Located under the external obliques, running in the opposite direction.

External abdominal oblique
Located on the side and front of the abdomen.

Rectus abdominis
Located along the front of the abdomen, this is the most well-known abdominal. Often referred to as the "six pack."

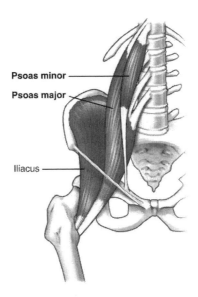

- **Psoas:** A dynamic stabiliser, this muscle links our trunk to our legs, working with the hip flexors. A weak, over-lengthened psoas can cause lower back pain and prevent cheerleaders from performing 'snapping' movements such as jumps, tucks and cradles. You can see if an athlete has a weak psoas muscle because they will have a slight curve in the lower back, with the backside sticking out.

- **Multifidus:** The multifidus is a very deep, long muscle that is aligned next to the spine. It helps the other core muscles stabilise the lower back and the pelvis before movement actually occurs. It anticipates the movement of the body and creates a sort of 'anchor' effect. Not using of the mutifidus puts strain on the other muscles and makes the athlete's effort harder than it needs to be, like trying to swim for safety without a lifejacket. Using the multifidus effectively requires athletes to find, recruit and train the muscle before strengthening. The first step is *finding it* and *being conscious of it* in order to engage and train it.

- **Pelvic Floor:** Similarly, the the pelvic floor (PFM) also acts as an invisible anchor. It is shaped like a nest of muscles that criss-cross in the basin of the pelvis. Its role is to support the bladder and reproductive organs, and if engaged and strengthen properly, it will help reduce pelvic tilt and other issues.

‣ **Obliques:** The obliques are much easier to train because they are easier to find and engage; they really help build a stronger 'trunk'. Instead of training just normal sit-ups, switching to a majority of twisting ab exercises is going to help strengthen the entire core. Some great aesthetic perks include working out your abs (which are working as a synergist) and shaping the areas around the hips.

Athletes require additional inner core training, but with an important notion: to effectively train the inner core muscles, movements need to be small and isolated. Strengthening the core is not about how many sit-ups one can do, but how isolated they can make the movement using only the psoas and TVA muscles - not by using abs, hip flexors, quads or the momentum of the movement.

EXPLAINING CORE TO ATHLETES

A weak core is the reason why many people have bad posture as well as lacking overall strength and stability. It's likely the reason why your athletes may not jump as high, achieve a tumble or stick their shape in a lib sequence. Imagine a tree in the wind, holding heavy branches and leaves: you want the trunk to be as strong as possible to sustain the weight and movement. Since abs are the outer part of the trunk, they won't help to be strong inside. The core is the middle part of your body where your arms and legs are connected and you stay strong during all your cheer skills.

‣ **Jumps:** Without a strong core, you might be able to lift and spring off the ground but you won't have the strength to snap the legs up and you may feel a disconnect between the upper and lower body.

‣ **Basing:** You heavily rely on your core to control the lift and feel your body move in conjunction with your arms and legs.

Also, your core will help to keep your posture, which means more control of the stunt.

▸ **Flying:** A flyer with a weak core is as useful as a chocolate teapot. If you have a weak core, you won't be able to perform the most basic skills like hold yourself up, ride baskets or pull shapes. Most problems you have with your flying can be fixed by having a stronger core.

▸ **Tumbling:** Even at beginner levels (with cartwheels, for example), if you have a weak core you will not be able to hold the hollow position (the building block of all tumbling passes).

FIXING CORE ISSUES

The core muscles are all slow twitch muscles, so as a consequence they are slow to fatigue. That means they can be trained on a daily basis, both while moving as well as stationary. To make the most of core muscles, athletes can use the 6 Cs:

▸ **Concentration:** Focusing the brain on the body part enhances proprioception (our ability to sense our body in motion). Conscious focus on movement enhances our body awareness.

▸ **Control:** Having a definite and positive impact on a body part by isolating and working the body's critical stability muscles. Ideal technique brings safe, effective results.

▸ **Centering:** Focusing on muscles that stabilise the pelvis and shoulder blades underlies the development of a strong core and enables the rest of the body to function efficiently. We must engage the core at a low level for extended periods of time.

▸ **Conscious breathing:** Belly in/belly out to activate deep stabilising muscles and to keep focused.

▸ **Core alignment:** A neutral position is key to proper alignment which leads to good posture.

▸ **Coordination:** Flowing movement results from brain and body working perfectly in synergy.

Engaging the core before every activity could alleviate 95% of all non structural back problems. To engage the core, pull the belly button to the back and squeeze the glutes. To effectively train the inner core muscles, and your athlete's awareness of them, there are four effective methods:

> ‣ **Strengthening through inversions:** Whereas doing endless core exercises may not be very appealing, a fun challenge can be introduced with 5 minutes of inversions during every training, which athletes can safely continue at home: handstands and headstands with added movement and strength progressions. The great thing about headstands is that they can be performed by all members of the team regardless of skill level or position.

> ‣ **Engage with a purpose:** Remind athletes of their core and the energy passing through their body so their upper and lower body feel fully connected. This will make the most of all their power and momentum.

> ‣ **Train small, isolated movements:** Strengthening the core is about isolated using only the psoas and TVA muscles (without

using rectus abdominis, hip flexors, quads or the momentum of the movement).

‣ **Tucking hips under:** Remind athletes to 'tuck their tails under' to ensure they align the spine, engage the pelvic floor, TVA and psoas muscles. This area might need additional training in the form of isolated, controlled movement of the inner core muscles.

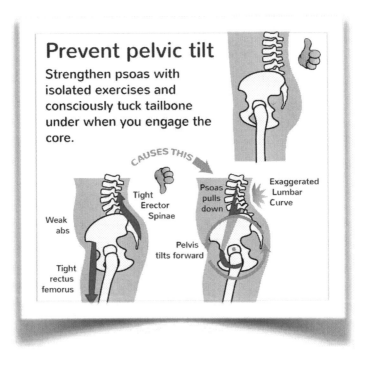

UPPER BODY

A weak upper body is another factor that limits many cheerleaders, especially in basing and tumbling skills. Even though the lower body has the larger muscles and provides the majority of the power and strength, movement cannot be fully stabilised unless there is enough strength in the upper body. Most cheerleaders find it difficult to perform basic arm conditioning, thinking mainly of their arms, forgetting to pay attention to train the muscles of the back. Even though the arms visibly perform the skill, the back provides the strength and support used by the arms.

EXPLAINING UPPER BODY TO ATHLETES

- **Jumps:** Without a strong upper body, you cannot keep good form and execute the correct technique. Because of this, it will be harder to keep the chest up, limiting your jump from going higher.

- **Basing:** Even though you should be lifting with your legs, your upper body will give you the strength to hold the flyer up and work with the legs to execute the lift. With a weak upper back and arms, it is harder to lock your arms out and keep the flyer stabilised above your head. It's the skeleton that should be taking the weight of the flyer, not the arms: if you can't lock out your arms you won't be able to distribute the weight of the flyer evenly throughout your body, causing difficulty and potential injury.

- **Flying:** A flyer with poor upper body strength is too heavy to lift. If you are being told that you are a 'heavy' flyer it likely has nothing to do with your weight. Some of the "lightest" flyers to lift actually weigh more on a scale because they have more muscles (which they use it to hold their weight through great technique). Sometimes smaller flyers feel heavier because they think they can rely on their size as opposed to holding themselves as they should. If you want to be a light flyer, stop worrying about your weight and make sure you work on your upper body strength.

‣ **Tumbling:** When tumbling, you often through the inverted position on your hands, meaning you are holding your body up with a combination of upper body and core strength. You need sufficient strength to be able to perform quality handstands to build to a higher difficulty level.

FIXING UPPER BODY ISSUES

‣ **Strengthening biceps:** Contraction of the bicep ensures stable movements where the arms need to squeeze and 'hit' quickly, such as motions and jumps. Practice strength and dynamic movements as well as drilling sharp arm positions. Dynamic arm training will help the upper body kinetic chains to be used to multi-directional force. For example: doing plenty of bicep curls with weights might be a great way to develop a good 'gun' show. But apart from getting your arm being good at flexing the bicep, how is this useful to cheer skills? If you're a base, you try to get your flyer up in one smooth vertical action. In reality, how many times does that happen? The reality is that the arms will work to counteract a movement that is not linear nor controlled, so this is what we need to train for. A great source of dynamic strength training ideas for arms can come from yoga or pilates, where strength and multidirectional movement is applied at the same time. This principle is the thought behind the STRENGTH and POWER workouts in the INTENSITY™ series.

‣ **Strengthening triceps:** You may assume the bicep is responsible for all your lifts in basing, however the tricep is the primary muscle used for lifting and extending (straightening) the arm, especially when in a lateral position. Exercises like tricep dips, pushups or one of the INTENSITY™ staple drills, the 'Ninja Sequence' are the easiest and most effective ways to train this muscle function. For maximum tricep engagement during stunting, remind bases and back spots to squeeze and engage their pinky fingers more than their index fingers so that the back of the arm can give more strength.

‣ **Strengthening deltoids:** Deltoids are the muscles of the upper arm and shoulders which help hold weight above the head (both as a base or inverted in a tumble). These muscles need a lot of endurance as well as power training to help push through the last 10% of the skill where we need to extended the arms.

‣ **Strengthening back:** The back is often neglected in cheer as its strength and utility are not as visible as the arms or pecs. The trapezius and latissimus dorsi that make up the primary muscles of the back serve as the fixator muscles for most stunting exercises, the power in a basket toss flick, as well as the inverted power for tumbling passes. Headstands, handstand jumps and INTENSITY™ drills such as the 'pointing dog' or the 'ninja sequence' inspired by pilates training are great exercises to strengthen the back.

‣ **Hyperextended arms:** A hyperextended joint naturally extends beyond optimal alignment. Some cheerleaders may have overextended joints and this can cause issues in execution as well as potential injury. It is important to keep an eye out for athletes with this issue so that their muscle memory can be trained to only extend to 90 or 95% of their full range of motion.

‣ **Shoulder flexibility:** The chest is an area that is over-trained in terms of strength in cheerleading (in comparison to the other areas) because most movements demand the involvement of the chest and lifting in front of the body. This is not necessarily an issue, but a lack of chest/shoulder stretching to compensate for the overuse in this area decreases shoulder flexibility. This causes issues such as bad posture and rounded shoulders that can hinder the movement in tumbling and basing. Chest stretches should be included at the end of every training session and athletes should know how to do this at home.

LOWER BODY

A good question to ask is: "Look at your arms. Now look at your legs. Which one has the bigger muscles?" Of course the answer is legs, yet so many athletes concentrate on using their arms when stunting and wonder why they find it difficult. Another issue is many athletes lack the ability to fully extend, engage and turn out the legs, which becomes the main inhibitor of developing good jumping skills.

EXPLAINING LOWER BODY TO ATHLETES

- **Jumps:** What goes up must go down, and to go up you must go down. To go up, you have to apply power and push off the floor with enough force and momentum to fully extend and propel you into the air. You cannot do this unless you bend down like a spring coil and use your full momentum, flicking your whole body off the floor by making full use of the mobility in your feet and toes. Your legs don't just need to be strong, they need to be fast and fully extended. Otherwise, you're like a puppet with all the strings loose.

- **Basing:** You cannot lift the flyer only with your arms. The arms and back only finish your movement which needs to start from the legs. Remember, what goes up must go down, and the opposite is also true: you need to go DOWN as much as you want your flyer to go UP. Focus your energy to push against the floor through your legs, core, upper body and then set the stunt with your upper body. There can be no lift without using the legs as the lifting effort should come 70% from the lower body and the core, with the upper body only assisting the effort and acting as a fixator to the movement.

- **Flying:** You need to use your leg power to aid the bases in the lifting process and create momentum. Try and load into your stunt without your back spot. You should be able to hold yourself here without their help. The back spot is not responsible to get you up. Their job is to alleviate weight off the bases, stabilise the stunt, and catch you. In your stunt, you may feel like your bases are drifting apart. It's your responsibility to bring them in: just squeeze your legs together and they will follow (playing the 'base accordion' drill is a fun way to put this theory into practice. Look out for this online and in our blog).

▸ **Tumbling:** As with basing and jumping, to go up, you must first push off. Forces are equal, so how far you go up is determined by how far you go down and push off. You should be able to perform most basic running tumbling such as round-offs and front handsprings from a lunge position. Don't rely on momentum created by running.

FIXING LOWER BODY ISSUES

▸ **Increasing speed in adductors:** Conditioning adductor speed will increase the snap in jumps and improve the landing. Most cheerleaders have weak adductors (remember it as 'add'-ing the legs back to starting position), but even those with strong adductors can suffer from slow speed. This is because they haven't been training plyometrics and explosive power. They usually have a higher ration of slow-twitch fibres and have concentrated mainly on strength and endurance instead.

Leg speed, not flexibility, is key.

SPEED!

(You only have 1 count!)

‣ **Foot and hip rotation:** Most cheerleaders jump with inverted (rolled-in) hips, causing the chest to fold forward and the tailbone to push back. As a result, the jump will be lower than it could be because the trajectory of the jump is not vertical and it is being stopped mid-height. Sadly, most cheerleaders need to have their muscle memory fully re-trained, and the work starts from the feet. The feet need to be fully pointed and heels rotated upward towards the ceiling. This will rotate the leg socket under in the hips and the chest will stay upright. Many traditional conditioning drills such as 'V-snaps', 'snaps-ups' are counterproductive because, even though they strengthen the adductors, they give improper muscle memory with the chest folding down towards the legs and the hips pushing back. To avoid this use kick drills, frog jumps or star snaps which encourage the hips to open and legs to snap up and down.

‣ **Pointing:** The amount of flexed feet in cheer is generally pretty shameful, still today. Not only is it aesthetically displeasing to look at, but allowing athletes to perform skills without first mastering eccentric contractions is completely counterproductive to their skill development. A foot that is not pointed adds to a leg which cannot be fully engaged. Ballet dancers and gymnasts spend their first years learning how to point and flex their feet; cheerleaders should be no different. Point work in the context of cheer should be an essential part of warmup and conditioning.

‣ **Increasing push-off:** The concept of Newton's 3rd law of motion can't be emphasised enough. In order to have lift-off, athletes first need to push off. This comes in two parts: dipping with legs and then using the full surface of the foot to flick off, finishing with the toes (just as we teach bases wrist action in a basket toss). A good cheer warmup will spend a large portion of time drilling push-off exercises, which are also a great way to increase the heart rate and endurance.

▸ **Keeping momentum:** A big issue with tumbling, jumping and basing is the loss of momentum through a 'dead' landing or catch. Athletes need to understand how to use the force against them to push back up. Instead of giving into the force, they can keep momentum going through controlled fluidity of movement: the movement never stops, the muscles and joints working as a spring, absorbing the weight set against them and pushing them back up. Performing plenty of rebound drills even after simple tumbles or jumps will improve muscular endurance and help the muscle memory to unconsciously rebound even at difficult times.

CONNECTIVE TISSUE

On a daily basis, cheer training can trigger a number of short-term and long-term issues on the joints. We often think of training our muscles, but whereas training the connective tissue that makes up the joints is often overlooked. Not paying enough attention to the integrity of our connective tissue can cause a number of ongoing issues and injuries. Our joints can be compromised by a number of factors:

▸ **Poor body mechanics:** Poor technique, posture and improper positioning will weaken the joint's stability, cause friction and overuse of certain muscle groups, tendons and ligaments.

▸ **Lack of strength and endurance:** Conditioned muscles will improve the joint's stability and alignment so that it equally distributes impact through the entire kinetic chain. Ensure that the joint does not have to overcompensate in order to cope with force or impact.

▸ **Poor flexibility:** This is just as significant as the strength and stability of the joint because it allows for a fuller range of motion in the event of an impact or trauma.

▸ **Overuse:** In all aspects of our sport, cheerleading training requires repetitive overhead movements with varying degrees of force, weight or impact. Avoiding repetition beyond what is necessary, and rotating skills can have a positive impact on reducing overuse injury rates.

‣ **Incorrect posture:** Poor posture will impact on alignment, having a direct role in causing excessive stress and overuse to the joint.

‣ **Lack of recovery:** With pressures of competing or achieving a skill, some athletes may want to train or compete on an existing injury, however mild or serious. Especially with the shoulder (which can become an impairment to the athlete's quality of life beyond cheerleading) we should leave enough recovery time for the joint to regain full stability and strength before training it again.

‣ **Long training breaks:** If an athlete has taken time off in between seasons or training sessions, they might be subject to "weekend athlete syndrome" when they get back. This causes a higher vulnerability to shoulder tendinitis since athletes are required to complete over head movement and the majority of the joint's cheer specific durability has been lost after having been off training.

‣ **Weight control:** Training within the appropriate weight range and ensuring the joints are not overloaded by bodyweight or external forces (stunt load, landing impact, etc..) is the best way to prevent joint stability issues. Progressive overload training is crucial to gradually improve the correct weight allowance on the joints.

‣ **Improper warm up:** Skills performed without sufficient warm up also put the joint at risk by the body temperature being too low for the synovial fluid to act as an effective layer of lubricant. Excessive stretching before explosive training and skills can weaken the muscles, ligaments and tendons which reduce the joint's stability.

‣ **Sudden strain or trauma:** There will be times where an athlete is confronted with an unexpected fall or bad landing. Even though all precautions can be taken to avoid the rate of these incidents, it is inevitable that freak accidents happen.

Optimal joint stability and total body fitness will have a significant impact on the body's ability to resist against the injury.

It may not seem like a priority to train our connective tissue as much as we train muscle strength and endurance. Injury prevention or rehabilitation aside, having strong or flexible connective tissue can also give us better mechanical efficiency. In simple words, less effort is required because we are evenly spreading forces throughout the entire kinetic chain.

Humans, like all living species, are incredibly sophisticated machines. It's hard to think of our bodies as machines but that's exactly how movement functions. This is why the study of human movement is called bio*mechanics*. In this spirit, we need to see our joints as levers. If you're not sure how levers work, this is a great time to look them up - there are three kinds.

In the body, **torque** (rotational) force is applied by pulling on a hinge to create a movement. This rotational force is created by a combination of all of our muscles contracting and relaxing around a joint. The joint itself acts as the **fulcrum** which creates the **pivot** motion. An easy way to think about this is to imagine a slot machine. The handle we pull is the lever. The torque force pivots around the nut. If the nut is loose, the mechanism will feel shaky and we can't apply force to it. If it's too tight, we may not be able to move it at all, and if we force the movement it will break.

The architecture, strength and elasticity of the connective tissue around the joints all contribute to the stability and the efficiency of the movement. A stable, strong joint creates a more even weight distribution across the kinetic chain. This means that the **lever** is stable so our muscles need to produce less effort and there is less chance of injury. Instead of thinking of our muscles as independent units, we need to think of the full kinetic chain: all elements are interdependent. If we have weak links in the chain, the exercise will be increasingly hard and the weakest link may snap. Therefore, training connective tissue is not just a way to prevent injury, but also a smart way to maximise strength and endurance.

It is worth noting that training and regenerating connective tissue takes 6-8 times longer than muscle tissue. If an athlete injures a tendon or ligament, it will take them six months to a year of rehabilitation before regaining full strength and mobility in the area.

The best way to train our connective tissue is through dynamic mobility training. **Dynamic mobility** can be described as training through constant change, movement, or progress. The goal is to get our joints to move comfortably in all directions, not just the directions they are meant to move. For example, let's say we are training a base to have better knee joint mobility. During a stunt, the base is meant to dip which can be trained through skill-specificity by doing lots of squats. This is a great way to get their dips better, but it won't help them become more resistant to an unexpected movement (if they slip or get a foot in the face) which causes their knee to move in a non-linear fashion. When mistakes happen they are not likely to happen with the right technique: this is the logic of dynamic mobility training. In this case, we would want to add in side lunges and squats at varying hip/foot angles: to train the knee joint in multi-directional movement, making it more resistant to the unexpected.

The term **optimal surplus** describes training beyond our required effort. We see this concept when training cardiovascular fitness, muscle strength and endurance, but this can also apply to training connective tissue. Essentially, we want to train our bodies to cope with more than is required so that our normal activities (a stunt, tumble or full out) become easier to execute and our bodies can cope with a margin of error when something goes wrong. Using progressive overload training combined with controlled dynamic activity is a great way to improve the mobility, stability and performance of our joints. For example, if some bases struggle with a rotation of the wrist you could include "rotating planks" as part of the conditioning (plank in a straight position, holding the weight on the hands, then perform circular motions in both clockwise and anticlockwise directions to the wrists' connective tissue) .

Training for optimal surplus should NOT, under any circumstance, mean that we should train through pain. The "no pain, no gain" philosophy is one that we must move away from: it is far from constructive. Acute pain is a sign that something is wrong. Pain is a defence mechanism that our bodies adopt to stop ourselves from harm so it makes no sense to push through it.

There is a difference, of course, between soreness and pain. Soreness can be a natural consequence of working hard and pushing through the barriers of progressive overload training. When we push beyond our comfort it is normal to feel some dull aching or mild burning of the muscles. Our body is at work and we can push through this as long as we can keep control of the movement. The discomfort should stop within a few seconds after we cease.

Pushing through a barrier can feel good: you are sore, but you feel like you have pushed yourself to a new level of success. Pain, on the other hand, is sharp and will continue after you cease the activity. At the first sign of sharp pain you should stop the activity immediately, rest and should the pain continue, consult a coach of physician before returning to regular activity.

6
CHEER SKILLS & TECHNIQUE

Technique. It's a word that is usually associated with coaches finger-wagging and athletes rolling their eyes in an "eat your broccoli" or "have you brushed your teeth?" fashion. We know it's good for us but it doesn't make it more exciting. Techniques are also varied depending on the style of cheerleading, the area we are from and the coaches we have worked with. Like a new hair stylist that look at our mane in disapproval, frowning at the work of the previous person's work (it comes with the job) opinions on techniques differ from person to person.

Instead of being stuck with certain ideals and ramming technique down athletes' throats, I like to present things to athletes using a different approach. Technique isn't good for you; **it gives you superpowers**. It's like having night-vision goggles when you're driving in the dark. It allows you to work at a mechanical advantage. It makes things easier on your body. You get to do more. It's a series of hacks that can transform your entire level of execution: but it requires an open mind and good self-awareness. Unlocking a desire to be a perfectionist when it comes to technique is the quickest way to cheerleading stardom, opening the doors to a whole new realm of possibilities - not just within cheer, but in other pursuits too.

BASING

Whether athletes are performing a simple or complex skill, these basic technique tips will help you maximise their potential, make it safer and make it easier. With adequate progression and enough conditioning, the only reason preventing a skill from hitting solidly is the body not working to its mechanical advantage. Technique is what fixes the mechanics so you need less effort to complete the an action. It's literally like learning to drive your car efficiently so that you use less gas.

ELEMENTS OF BASING

SAFETY

The flyer's head is the most important body part to protect. Aside from falling, many flyers are getting injured *after* being caught. This is because bases are not fully absorbing or controlling the dismount appropriately, thinking that the flyer is now "out of danger." We can avoid this by drilling impact-absorbing catching drills and reminding athletes to finish a stunt even stronger than when it started.

LEGS

Legs have larger muscle groups. Therefore, the majority of the effort should come from the legs, channelled to the upper body via correct alignment and the core. Arms should only be used to stabilise and finish the inertia of the movement. Sometimes this will be a concept that athletes, especially newcomers, struggle to fully grasp. The focus naturally goes to the arm because it makes contact with the flyer.

Overcome this by getting athletes to experience the difference between using arms and legs together vs arms alone. Say "let's try this stunt without using legs," then "let's try this stunt with a little leg dip" and finally, "now let's try the stunt with full focus on the legs and drive up through the core." When this is complete, ask them to compare/ explain the difference they found.

How low an athlete can go is not the goal: it's *power and momentum* that counts. Dipping too low, especially when the hips dip below the knees decreases the ability to spring back up again. Think about the timing, power and momentum of the dip. Another key is to look at the *other* foot (not the one you are holding) to keep good rhythm and synchronisation. Having just one of these small details out of place or at the wrong time can reduce the potential of the entire movement.

In the long term, warm ups for bases should include plenty of dynamic squats using strong technique so that they develop the muscle memory to dip low and stand up fast.

POSTURE

Bad posture (over-arching or rounding out) can cause lower back injuries and is one of the main reasons why bases find stunts more difficult than they should be. A good posture will align the stunt's centre of gravity to the base of support so that the momentum flows straight from the ground to the top of the movement. Good posture will also make a stunt more stable once it's reached the top.

Instead of being a posture nag, I like to remind athletes by poking gentle fun at them such as "we should have no grandmas or ducks doing the basing," opting instead to "think like a tree" or "tuck your tails under" (whatever works for you). Giving them a feeling of what a strong posture should *feel* like is just as important as showing or telling them. When in load position or drilling stunts where it is safe to manipulate athletes, I like to gently press the small of their backs, reminding them to "tuck their tails under," or roll their shoulders back whilst pressing the palm of my other hands between their shoulder blades.

Drilling good posture through strengthening the TVA on a regular basis will make basing much more comfortable, and will be safer for the flyers. It also gives one of the best tools to develop core alignment strength. Also it gives them an opportunity to be reminded of what their body should feel like when holding weight - regardless if they are upside down or basing. If you train headstands as part of your conditioning - remind bases to use their 'headstand mode' when basing.

GRIPS

Grips need to be strong but also fluid. If a grip is stiff (especially in baskets), muscles become more vulnerable to injury. It also leaves little room for grip adjustment to fix the stunt if needed. Explore grip techniques which give the wrist relief and flexibility so that the full skeleton holds the weight of the flyer as opposed to one joint. Stability should come from the foundations, not the grip. The grip itself should be an extension of the structure's strength.

DISMOUNTS

The biggest nemesis of dismounts is catching low, so drilling bases to catch as high as possible will increase the time of contact with the flyer and give more control. This will make the stunt cleaner and reduce the chances of the flyer hitting the ground as the base will have more time to react to the downwards force.

Another issue with dismounts are 'dead' catches (ie. the 'thud' sound that comes when bases catch without absorbing). Catching stiff causes huge impact on the joints and is also the cause of bruises. The best way to prevent athletes from turning into blue dalmatians is to drill how to absorb the impact. Rather than halting the momentum of the mass, the bases should slow down the momentum, absorbing and controlling the mass. Imagine what would happen if you suddenly had to stop a car in an emergency. The jolt itself will cause excessive wear on the vehicle mechanics and the car wouldn't last long if all it did all day was emergency stops. The same goes for the body. A car needs to slow it's approach to a complete stop, and cheer dismounts should be the same.

We strive for low impact, no bruises and no injury. To achieve this, athletes need to maintain a strong posture by engaging the core upon impact and absorbing the fall using the legs to slow down the velocity.

BACK BASES/BACK SPOTS

Back spots lift the flyer by 'pulling up'. This seems like a perfectly normal thing to do until we look at the muscles behind this action. Pulling up engages the trapezius, deltoids and biceps as the primary muscles. Instead, *pushing up* to activate the tricep the largest muscle in the arm) will hugely reduce the effort required to lift and stabilise a stunt. To help with this, make back spots more aware of the difference. By trying a simple load-in, squeezing the grip with their pinky and ring fingers instead of their thumb and index fingers. Contracting the pinky will activate the tricep muscles instead of the biceps. You can also try this without a stunt. Simply hold your hands out like you were holding candlesticks and alternate between squeezing the thumb/index fingers (bicep contracts) or the pinky/ring fingers (tricep contracts). Once this is clear, back spots can easily push up with the backs of their arms instead of strenuously lifting through their biceps.

Pushing up with pinkies high uses the stronger tricep muscles.

Another advantage for the back spot is to widen the stance of the feet. It creates a more stable base of support and lowers their centre of gravity, giving more strength and stability.

STAYING CLOSE TOGETHER

Staying close and aligning the skeleton ensures that the momentum comes from under the stunt rather than from opposing sides. A fully vertical push will give more power to the stunt. As a result, it will go up more easily and with more stability.

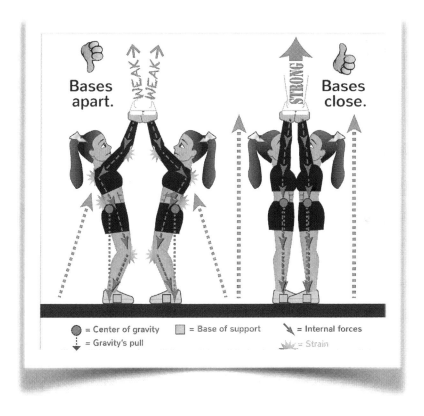

FRONT BASES

Although they may not always be used, front bases can be helpful for additional safety. Think of your front spot as an additional stabiliser who can also reduce the strain on the bases' wrists (a little bit like the training wheels on a child's first bicycle). When front basing, it's best to leave the ankle grip to the back spot, and focus instead on supporting the grip or wrists of the bases. Another way to help, is by cupping just below the flyer's knees to prevent them from falling forwards. Just make sure the support goes upwards rather than backwards. One of the best uses for a front base is to reduce the velocity of the flyer coming down to the ground by absorbing the impact from the front.

COMMON BASING ISSUES & FIXES

‣ **Clunking heads:** Also known as the 'cheer kiss,' this can be pretty dangerous so it shouldn't be considered a funny incident. This phenomenon happens when the bases catch a cradle with bad posture and forces bring the torso forward, causing the heads to bump together. Luckily there is an easy fix to prevent this: better engagement of the core muscles and making sure the bases are absorbing the impact with their legs. Sometimes the force can be so strong that even if the catch is controlled, the force still brings the bases' heads dangerously together. In this case, once the bases have made contact with the flyer and intimated the catch, they can turn their heads towards flyer's feet to create distance between the heads.

‣ **Small pop/dip:** If the dismount pop is small, it is because of one or more of the following: poor timing, weak leg dip, tired rebound, arms collapsing, unstable core or lack of a shoulder shrug. Repeating bad pops can be dangerous, so it's better to film the dismount, slow down the video to zone in on the area that needs more work, then layer instructions to gradually increase power or strength. To fix this long-term, quality squats and handstand jumps will build power in the legs, shoulders and arms that can then be applied to basing dismounts

‣ **Weak backing:** Often, the back spot may not be giving as much support as they could because they are lifting with their biceps rather than pushing up with their triceps (this can be fixed with the 'pinky hack' described previously). Switching back spots between stunt groups during training will highlight if a back spot is making enough effort or taking a back seat. Remind back spots that they should be using their legs and dipping just as much as the bases, so squats and tricep dips are great conditioning exercises to keep back spots at the top of their game.

‣ **Falling forwards:** If the flyer is falling forwards during a smush or reload, the front base needs to give further support and stabilisation by cupping the flyer below the knees and slowing down the descent.

‣ **Weak preparation:** The set of the stunt (such as the clap or getting into position) will predetermine the success of the skill. Making a strong, confident entrance to the stunt will set the tone and make sure athletes are confident, powerful and focused.

‣ **Low energy:** Low energy can be due to a loss of stamina, overheating, poor nutrition, hydration, or muscle fatigue among many other reasons. It can also be a result of athletes not using correct technique and body positions, forcing them to overuse the wrong muscles. Determine the reason for the low energy to find the right fix by looking at the lines of movement and if they are using a mechanical advantage.

‣ **Bent legs:** If the bases' legs are overly bent when they are holding up the stunt, they need to be reminded to push their feet to the ground and squeeze from their glutes all the way to their toes. Isometric strength conditioning can also help stabilise the base's stance.

‣ **Bent arms/collapse:** When the bases are not able to hold up the flyer, it's probably because they are trying to hold the stunt up using their arm muscles and joints instead of relying on an aligned skeleton and a strong core. It could also be due to their fatigued arms from taking too much of the effort during the lifting action, leaving them little strength to hold the stunt up. Timing, strength, proper form and co-ordination all come into play ultimately save more power for when it's needed and keeping the stunt solid until the dismount.

▸ **Low catching:** Low catching is usually a result of a weak pop that doesn't give the bases enough reaction time to locate the flyer in the air before making contact. It can also be a result of a lazy catch, poor core control or a 'dead' catch. If these persist they need to be addressed immediately, as low catching will cause lower back/shoulder injury for the bases or can result in the flyer falling through. Ensure that the bases have a enough upper body and core strength to catch and that they are using the legs to absorb with control.

FLYING

Flyer skills are different from many of the basing skills as they mainly require isometric contractions (holding shape/body position in the air) and arm/core strength for stability in loads. They need much less dynamic movement from the legs (dipping and squatting) after the initial load unless they are performing high level and/or creative skills. Flyers often struggle to hit stunts because their isometric skills are mostly trained at home, on the ground or on a stunt trainer and rarely trained with added elements of physical stress (i.e. in anaerobic conditions, at a high heart rate or with muscle fatigue). Whereas bases can compensate bad technique with strength, flyers rely much more on technique and joint stability.

Flyers also affect their mass during the catching phase of the stunt. Mass is not a flyer's weight, but the force of the flyer's body plus momentum at impact with the bases. This can be controlled by distributing the mass evenly in a tight isometric contraction of the whole body. A flyer who is fully contracted has a more stable centre of motion than a flyer with little control. No matter how small or light the flyer may be, it's the centre of motion which keeps moving. The more stable the centre of motion and the more the weight is distributed throughout the contact surface, the less heavy a flyer will feel to the bases.

Height, more than weight, is important with flyers because their height determines how far their centre of gravity is from the ground. Shorter flyers have a lower centre of gravity and therefore make the stunt easier to control. This is not to say taller girls shouldn't fly, but additional height will require more stability from the entire stunt group.

Flying also requires performance skills and choreographed movements which need to be embedded in muscle memory before they are attempted in a routine. One of the ways I like to help flyers is getting them to visualise the level of control and how to hit counts. I tell them to imagine that on every count, a photograph is being taken and they need to squeeze tight on every count so that they all look the same and there are no blurry areas on the photograph.

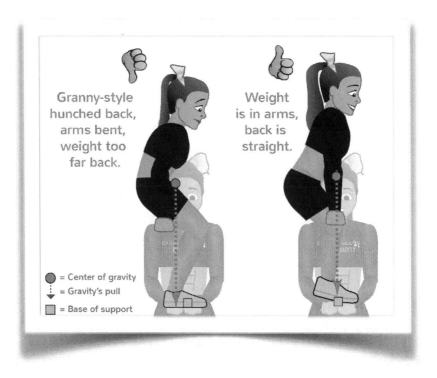

Granny-style hunched back, arms bent, weight too far back.

Weight is in arms, back is straight.

⬤ = Center of gravity
↓ = Gravity's pull
⬛ = Base of support

Flyers need to develop their stop-start technique and learn to squeeze isometrically on every move. For young flyers, I love using the 'Starfish/Jellyfish' drill that I came up with when teaching my first batch of minis. It's a great conditioning game that they love, plus it's very helpful to get them to understand the basics of isometrics. Get the athletes to lie down on the mat in a 'spread eagle' fashion, telling them to be wobbly and relaxed like a jellyfish. Then, when you say 'starfish,' they need to tighten up their bodies, squeezing their fists in a High V, legs straight, toes pointed and backs flat to the ground. Then repeat by saying 'starfish' - 'jellyfish' a few times until the conditioning has done its work. Remind them to keep their head neutral, back against the floor and keep their arms up in a High V, not in front. Doing this drill with young athletes on a regular basis is fun for them but it is also a great way to give them a simple verbal cue when they are in the air. If they are 'jellyfishing' in a stunt - saying 'starfish!' is usually all they need for them to correct themselves. This drill can be used in a variety of ways and shapes, both lying down or standing.

ELEMENTS OF FLYING

LOADS / MOUNTS

When in the load position, inexperienced flyers tend hunch their back, keep weight on their feet, and/or keep their hips too low/far behind them. A fun way to help them visualise the correct position is reminding them to be a 'chicken', not a 'grandma':

- ‣ Perk up and look ahead
- ‣ Hold weight on the arms
- ‣ Align shoulders, elbows, hands, knees
- ‣ Back straight or with a slight curve down
- ‣ Hip height should be between the shoulders and the knees

Test if their load position is correct by drilling it without a back spot (staying in the load, not going all the way up). This is a very effective way to show the flyer that the back spot is not there to help them up; instead their role is to help the bases and stabilise the stunt. Until the flyer can fully load and hold their own weight without the back spot, they should not be allowed to go up as this will cause the bases unnecessary fatigue and exposure to a possible fall.

STUNT CHECKLIST

- ‣ Squeeze fists to help the isometric contraction of the entire arm. Positions may vary depending on style and choreography, but when in the classic 'High V' position, flyers should imagine they are holding themselves up on an invisible handlebar. They should focus on creating a triangle of tension between the two fists and the middle of the chest (the sternum) as three points of a triangle.
- ‣ Shoulders should be kept down and slightly closed in, neutral spine position by facing forward, chin down but not excessively.

> ▸ Their gaze should be ahead or slightly up, looking at a fixed object in the distance. Looking down will cause them to shift their centre of mass, making the stunt more likely to fall. Even worse, it makes them project towards the ground, which tempts them to bail out of their stunt.

> ▸ The flyer should avoid adjusting the stunt, as this will only shift their centre of mass, making the bases' job more difficult. Instead, ask flyers to squeeze. White-horse coaching is extremely important here: favour quick, visual and verbal cues that will prompt them to autocorrect (Jellyfish/headstand position/squeeze/tail under etc). This will help to control their centre of mass and fix the stunt's centre of gravity.

> ▸ Keep hips square and tuck the tailbone under by squeezing, rotating the pelvis upwards.

> ▸ Straighten the knees. Most times, flyers may think that their legs are straight, so instead of getting into a mid-air debate, ask them to pull up and push knees to the back wall.

- Feet need to be fully flat. The more the weight is distributed equally on the contact surface, the easier it is to lift or hold than if the pressure is concentrated in one area. Remember: black horse coaching such as "stop toeing" will have the exact opposite effect that you are looking for. Make sure you 'white horse' the instruction to avoid the stunt entering a tug-o-war or collapsing.

- Give priority to training speed, power, stability and isometrics rather than just focusing on flexibility. A flyer's ability to perform a skill with speed and control will be safer, neater and score more points than performing a more flexible skill executed slowly and with less control. Think of flexibility as being the icing on the cake rather than the cake itself. The icing makes it look great, but if you're all icing and no cake e you'll have no substance and look like a mess.

DISMOUNTS

- In a toss or cradle, the flyer needs to hold their position, squeezing as they wait for the pop. They shouldn't try to initiate the cradle or snap until they hit the top of the cradle. Their focus should be entirely on keeping a strong isometric contraction to get as much height as possible.

- Ride up with arms and shoulders, lifting up.

- Ride the pop all the way, snapping into shape or cradle only when hitting at the very top. Shifting shape will inhibit the upwards trajectory, reducing the height of the cradle.

- Keep hands clean to the sides, squeezing into the body. Usually, I like to discourage flyers from catching themselves with their arms around the bases shoulders and the back spot throwing their fists through to catch the underarms. Opt instead for the back spot to use a 'butterfly' style catch (where the back spot catches the flyer with hands flat across the flyer's shoulder blades). Even though this may seem more daunting for beginners, it gives the stunt more control, causes less bruising, fewer elbows in faces and helps flyers to concentrate on staying tight in their cradle. In addition, flyers will develop the correct muscle memory to progress to more difficult dismounts which could be lethal with arms out. Reversing this habit once it's embedded in the long-term memory will be painful both physically and mentally! If the cradle or dismount requires the flyer to catch themselves, the movement needs to be small, neat and controlled to prevent clashing of limbs with the bases.

▸ A relaxed or piked cradle is unpredictable and heavy to catch, becoming unsafe for the entire stunt group. Tell your flyers they can lose pounds simply by staying tight and tucking their tails under (sadly, this trick will not work on a scale or when trying on a new dress). Toes need to be pointed from the ride up to the end, ankles welded together and quads engaged, actively squeezing adductors together. This will help the body fully contract, allowing the smallest pike angle possible. This will keep the centre of mass more stable and evenly distribute the mass across the entire body.

FLYING TECHNIQUE

Regardless of the skill level, most flying problems fall under the same category and are caused by the same usual suspects: core, stability, isometrics, and mass distribution.

> ‣ **Lethargic performance:** A lethargic performance is caused by poor body control and low awareness of isometric contractions. Train the hollow position with headstands and shapes when fatigued, achieving good control before putting skill in a stunt. Try the starfish-jellyfish drill and cue. Boost flyers with confidence and the desire to show off.

> ‣ **Bent legs:** This can be caused by a lack of lifting action, not pushing the knees back, not contracting the muscles or engaging the core, thus breaking the extension of the hip and knee joints. Ensure the flyer is fully stable and confident with the skill before they try it in the air, then help them to fix the kinetic chain by asking them to lock their hips and push their knees backwards.

> ‣ **Collapse:** When a flyer collapses or bails, it could be due to a confidence issue or because they are looking down. The flyer needs to be stable and confident about performing the skill in the air, so it's good to allow them enough progression time to perfect skills at post (staying tight with legs together when the flyer is in a single leg skill) before moving onto training shapes.

> ‣ **Tendency to pike:** This happens in a dismount when the flyer's hips push back into a piked position. They might be attempting a hollow position but performing it incorrectly by not fully extending the hip joint. Drilling exercises such as cradle snaps (a staple drill of the INTENSITY™ workout) and headstands are a great way to condition muscle memory. In the early days of learning cradles, I like to teach the 'banana snap' technique in the air just to help athletes bring the hips forward, extend that joint fully and train their basic muscle memory.

This is the 'cradle snap' drill modified for the air. Initially, this means that the flyer will ride up in a high clasp and stay strong (ankles tight together too). At the height of the pop, the arms come down hard by the sides as the hips come forward, with a deliberate contraction of hips and arms. The 'banana' part (with the hands clasped to the top) can be weaned off as the snap is embedded in the muscle memory. That, or you could be reading this book in the future when the 'banana-snap-cradle' has become the standard! See this drill on the cheerobics.net blog.

▸ **Slow speed:** Slow execution can be caused by lack of confidence, anticipating the skill or lack of dynamic power. Sadly, there is no quick fix for this (energy drinks won't help right now). Instead, this needs a lot of plyometric and power work, two or three times a week for at least 6 weeks to see a noticeable difference in the reaction time. The conditioning focus should be on skill-specific power drills for the selective recruitment of fast-twitch muscles as well as the building of muscle memory to quicken the reaction time. Start with a low range of motion to build confidence and gradually increase it, keeping the same speed or music BPM (beats per minute).

▸ **Feet apart:** Flyers might be relying on their bases to keep their feet together, even though this is fully in the flyer's control. Of course, you can train hip flexors, glutes, adductor strength so that flyers are able to pull bases together, increasing the chances of the stunt staying up. However, my favourite way to fix this is a fun little game called 'base accordion'. This is fairly simple and safe if the stunt group is stable in a prep. The flyer gets into prep and starts pushing their feet out, forcing bases to step back. Then they squeeze their legs together, forcing the bases back in. Repeating this a few times will make the flyer look like they are playing 'base accordion' with their legs helping the flyer understand that the distance between their feet is within their control. The next time the flyer's feet are too far apart, all they need is a reminder to squeeze their ankles in by using words like 'squeeze in' or 'accordion.' They will be much more reactive in keeping their ankles tight and together.

Flyers: Squeeze legs in to help bases.

JUMPS

Jumps are often neglected in comparison to other cheer skills. For a number of reasons, jump training can often fall on the back burner until it's time to put the routine together. However jumps can easily be transformed and add points to the scoresheet by improving technique without necessarily increasing difficulty. By having a jump section which is well drilled, your team could earn a number of extra points on the scoresheet that may be easier to achieve as a team than in other skill sections.

The first myth to abolish is that jumps are about flexibility. Flexibility is required, of course, but even a very limited range of motion can translate into a great jump. A very flexible athlete can also have terrible jump height. This is because when it comes to jumps speed and power have more importance than flexibility. An athlete can only reach a range of motion within a certain timeframe. If their movement is slow, they can't even reach half of their full range of motion. Hyperflexibility only matters once the athlete has achieved their full range of motion. Once this is achieved, they can work their flexibility by increasing speed and power.

JUMP TECHNIQUE

Jump technique comes in many forms (i.e. counts, arm placement and set) but they all have one thing in common: execution and uniformity is the holy grail and the pitfall of so many teams. When all other scores are very close, the jump section is where a team can really bag some extra points.

Fundamentally, a level 1 toe touch and a level 6 toe touch should not look any different when it comes to execution. What *should* differ is the complexity of the jump sequence as a whole. Jumps seem to be the 'poor cousin' of the cheer skills that end up being inadequately trained.

Comparing training methods with many teams over the years, good jumps can be narrowed down to three sacred rules to training jumps. Even a team of complete beginners can get decent jumps in 3 months.

THE THREE SACRED RULES OF JUMP TRAINING

1) **Train weekly, but for no more than 5 minutes.** Training jumps for longer will decrease the explosive power. Training fatigued jumps will only train poor technique in the muscle memory. You may think the extra time spent is beneficial, but it's counterproductive to training speed and power. Jumps should not be trained back-to-back for five minutes at a time. Instead they should be staggered to allow enough recovery time between sequences.

2) **Jump with the upper body.** Before training athletes on jump choreography, ensure they have a strong T jump with a good **triple extension** (when hips, ankles and knees are fully extended). Ensure hips are forward, toes pointed, shoulders back and arms strong. Train this for at least a few weeks before allowing any add ons or skill variations. Think of this as the cheer equivalent of the *Karate Kid*'s "wax on, wax off' principle: muscle memory drills at their finest. Training the upper body to stay strong and the legs to pushoff with power builds a strong foundation before adding in skill. This type of training has three benefits. First, it reduces the need to correct all those "keep chest up" comments that pollute our scoresheets. Second, you will get extra execution points by creating a visual cheat: even if your legs are not very high, all chests are up and arms are level so jumps will look much higher. Last, even if it might seem like a slow start to training, it gives the body a mechanical advantage by training upward trajectory, and hips, legs and feet will be at their optimum to tackle the next variations and progressions.

3) Train speed & power, not flexibility. Many coaches and athletes are concerned that their flexibility is too poor for jumps. I ask them to sit in a straddle on the floor with their toes pointed, backs straight and arms out in a T. Anyone with minimal mobility can do this easily. I proceed to tell them if they can do that, they have enough flexibility for a good jump. Hyperextension will come with time but is not necessary. What is needed, however, is that they learn how to speed up the process between their triple extension at lift-off (legs, hips, ankles, toes fully extended), their 'hit' position at the top, and snapping their legs back together. This process has nothing to do with flexibility. Instead, it involves the speed of the fast-twitch muscles, the power within your connective tissue of your joints and the overall reaction speed of the kinetic chain. Starting by training in short daily bursts, week by week you will add 1-2cm to your jump height until you reach the same straddle position you had on the floor. **Train athletes to think in speed, not height.**

Jumps with poor height will be scored much higher if toes are pointed, arms are placed correctly, chest is up, and if it is performed with uniform timing as a team; a slightly higher jump but with poor execution scores lower. Team uniformity with good technique will always score higher than a mixed team with a few very good jumpers at the front, but where all other arms, legs and chests are in disarray. This is the strategy that I have always used and that has served me well, especially when dealing with a less experienced team.

THE JUMP CHECKLIST

Step 1 - Preparation: Whether it's a clap, High V or choreographed, the prep will set the tone for the jump. It needs to be full of control, speed, strength and confidence to prepare the rest of the body to follow.

Step 2 - Charge: The more powerful the dip, the higher the rebound. Athletes can imagine their legs as springs. The more you pull down (i.e. bend your legs), the more powerful the release. The movement needs to be fluid, with no awkward body positions that kill momentum. Arms need to give lift and stability to the upper body, increasing the overall velocity of the upward movement.

Step 3 - Jump: Explode upward through the legs, pushing off against the floor by using the full foot, flicking off with the toes. This will make the best use of the achilles tendon, which is the body's natural spring. Legs need to squeeze together with hips, knees and ankles fully locked out and toes pointed to get maximum height. This is what we call a triple extension.

Step 4 - HIT: This is a time for multitasking, which can only be drilled through muscle memory and rapid muscle sequencing. This technique might feel strange at first, and athletes may struggle to get to their usual height for a few weeks when switching over from traditional methods. After the initial adjustment, the jump potential will improve far beyond what could have been achieved otherwise.

> ‣ Hit your motion HARD, squeezing in an isometric contraction at the very top. We recommend a T or candlesticks as a motion, because lower motions (such as a Low V) have a tendency to bring the chest down.
>
> ‣ Keep the gaze at eye level or higher.
>
> ‣ Keeping the chest up starts with...the toes! A strong turn-out will rotate the leg joints outwards in the hip socket, which will help the hips tuck under and keep the chest up.
>
> ‣ Squeeze and tuck the tailbone under. Ensure legs go out to the side rather than to the front to avoid pushing the hips back.
>
> ‣ Open up the chest and squeeze shoulder blades together whilst hitting a motion forwards. This will prevent shoulders

from rounding forward during the jump which will cause the chest to drop.

▸ Snap the jump shape back in at the top of the jump, remembering to focus on speed of hitting and snapping back down.

Step 5 - Land: Control the landing by absorbing the floor and squeezing into the centre of your body. Use the momentum to spring back up for the next jump to avoid killing the momentum.

Step 6 - Clean: At the end of the jump sequence, clean by squeezing in towards the core.

Rebound Jumps: When performing multiple jumps in sequence, use the full downward momentum of the jump with a fluid dip and rebound, pushing off against the ground. Focus on jumping up and hitting the triple extension before snapping into the shape again.

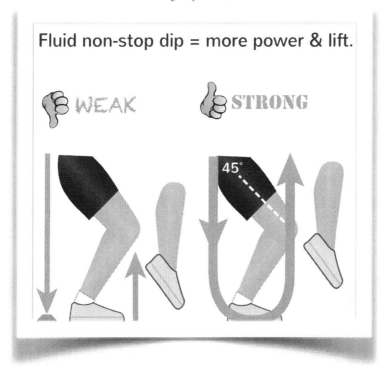

JUMPING ISSUES & FIXES

▸ **Weak preparation/arms:** The preparation will determine the power and technique of the jump. Make sure the athletes have a confident, powerful T-jump and triple extension with all points of technique before they go on to perform a more difficult jump.

▸ **Lethargic execution:** If the execution is lethargic, it is because they are not contracting their legs, core, and/or arms enough. They are being a 'jellyfish'. Look at training isometric and eccentric strength through targeted exercises and by training T-jumps to a suitable power before adding more complexity to the jump.

▸ **Bent legs:** If the athletes are bending their legs on takeoff, they are not engaging their leg muscles and fully springing upward with a triple extension, or flicking the tip of their toes off the ground. Limp, flexed feet will cause knees to bend, because they are linked to the same kinetic chain which gets interrupted if there is not an isometric contraction. Drilling kicks, T-jumps and giving constant reminder to point the toes, feeling a squeeze from the glutes is key.

‣ **Chest rolling forwards in toe touch:** This is a combination of a bad turnout, hips under-rotating and weak upper body strength. General conditioning exercises such as front and side kicks or partner-assisted jumps will help develop good technique. Focus should be on leg extension, turnout and tucking hips under. A great cue is also a simple "roll your shoulders back".

‣ **Messy landing:** A messy landing is due to poor control, collapsing when they reach the ground. Encourage athletes to control their energy, absorb and squeeze into the landing before snapping up to 'clean'. One of my favourite drills is aimed at correcting this. It's called *'Clean or Die'* - athletes lie down in two rows (in windows) facing each other and with their hips in line, about 1 foot from each other. One row 'cleans' on odd counts while the other row snaps out in a star, then in even counts they swap. The close proximity means they must be very precise and quick with their snapping - otherwise they collide. Hence 'clean or die'. (Disclaimer: athletes might get a few bruises, all in the name of good drilling fun.)

‣ **Low height & speed:** Slow speed occurs when there is insufficient power in the muscles that control the triple extension. For a toe touch this includes the hip flexors, adductors and psoas. Even with good flexibility, a lack of power of these muscles will make it difficult for the athlete to perform the 'snap' required for the jump to hit. Power training and skill-specific drills such as jump kicks are an excellent way to isolate and improve this particular issue.

‣ **Poor flexibility:** Before deciding if flexibility is the real issue or if it's speed related, it's best to check the athlete's floor flexibility. If their maximum range of motion is similar to their jump range, then they will need to improve flexibility by working on this daily for at least 4 weeks. Otherwise, refer above to the 'low height & speed' recommendations.

TUMBLING

Tumbling is a solo skill that does not depend on other teammates: the athlete is solely responsible for the development of their own skill and execution. This is why it is so important that the athlete goes through each repetition and progression with great care from the very start of the cognitive and associative phase of learning. Athletes that progress to the autonomous stage of learning with improper technique are not only risking their safety, they are completely compromising their longterm goals.

There is often a divide between the gymnastics and cheerleading schools of thought when it comes to tumbling. Even though the skills are the same between the two disciplines compared to gymnastics, cheerleaders rush progressions, which can be frustrating to a purist gymnastics coach. Equally, on the cheerleading side, there can be a frustration towards gymnastics because the methods tend to take so long to implement, it would be impossible to progress through the cheerleading levels within the timeframe required (unless you're an elite gymnast already). Who is right?

We can also ask what comes first, the chicken or the egg? It's a question of circumstance and priority. Are we after an egg today or a chicken tomorrow? Yes, within cheerleading you can progress your skills faster than you would with gymnastics, but there is a bigger risk of injury and developing bad technique if the rush is too fast, causing irreparable damage to the muscle memory. With gymnastics, the process is so thorough that it builds an athlete almost cell by cell, which will decrease the injury probability but of course, this takes lots of time. Like with all things, it's not about right or wrong but it's a question of finding the right balance. Gymnastics *needs* to be so precise because there often is a hairline margin between first and second place. Skill precision within gymnastics is so important; individual athletes are under the microscope and a level of near-perfection is almost a requirement. Within cheerleading, even though execution is important both for safety and the scoresheet, it is more acceptable for the skills to be rougher around the edges. Cheerleading is more accepting of imperfect tumbling execution because it's more of a 'jack-of-all-trades' type of sport. Its variety and inclusiveness is what makes it one of the fastest growing sports. Saying that, there is nothing stopping us from refining our execution, especially when it comes to tumbling. Each individual tumble skill would have its own guidelines for execution, but all share the same platform of technical guidelines.

GENERAL TUMBLING TECHNIQUE

- **Feet:** Actively squeeze the knees and ankles together.

- **Legs:** Straighten the legs, contracting then fully extending through a solid push off the floor using the entire foot, flicking off with the toes.

- **Hips:** Keep hips square, passing through the handstand position. In tumbles that require flexion of the hips (tucks, pikes, etc.) pay special attention to engaging the core (mainly psoas and the TVA)

- **Trunk:** The chest should stay up and strong (think of puffing up like a proud penguin).

- **Arms & shoulders:** Arms and shoulders should be straight, but athletes should absorb the impact with the shoulders, not the elbow joint which is much weaker. Especially with athletes who have hyperextended elbows, pay extra attention so that the force does not push them beyond their range of motion. Encourage a slight bend in the elbow to absorb the impact (a lesson I wish I had learned when training in kickboxing, before I decided to execute ridge strike with a straight arm. Ouch.)

- **Head:** The head should be in a neutral position to give the spine correct alignment. This is a common mistake that causes bigger issues. Athletes need to keep their chins down. A great way to drill this is making use of a good chin block to tactically reinforce the neutral head positioning. There is an excellent product, the *Perfect-a-Flip*, which was designed for this very purpose and is highly recommended.

Tumble with your head neutral.

During the setting and landing phases of the tumble, the same technique applies as for jumps: the prep needs to set the tone for the skill. It needs to be full of control, speed, strength and confidence to prepare the rest of the body. Dip low and spring back up to get maximum height and velocity, keeping the momentum going and using the full surface of the foot to flick off the ground. Land by absorbing the impact and squeezing into a clean, static position to control the full momentum.

TUMBLING TECHNIQUE ISSUES & FIXES

Feet apart: This is a common issue in tumbling that can create a variety of problems from lack of power to crooked tumbling to serious injuries (particularly in the knees). Many athletes have a difficult time feeling that their feet are apart. One way to correct this is to increase their adductor strength by actively squeeze the big toes together as a focus point to build muscle memory. A fun conditioning drill for this is playing team relay games where athletes race by jumping with a beanbag or small object between their legs and knees. It's a team game that is not only great fun and can be very effective at drilling adductor muscle memory. Cueing 'beanbag' is then enough to trigger the athlete's corrective abilities when training their tumbling.

Bent legs: Most athletes have bent legs because they don't have the strength or awareness to fully engage the glutes, quads, hamstrings or VMO muscle (on the inside of the leg, by the knee) nor do they push off with the full surface of the foot. Strengthening those muscle groups will develop better body awareness and help them perform their skills with tight, strong legs.

Arms bending on contact with the floor: Even though we don't want the elbow joint to be 100% extended, having bent arms is also a big issue. This could be caused my limited shoulder flexibility, weakness in deltoids and trapezius or poor wrist strength/mobility. Stretching the pectorals and increasing the upper back strength of the athlete will help open up their shoulder mobility. Increasing the strength of the deltoids and trapezius will also help stabilise the overhead position. The perfect cure for this is a good dose of handstand jumps as a part of every warmup.

Not passing through a handstand position: (arching, piking down): A handstand is the building block of tumbling. Nearly every tumbling skill passes through a handstand position. Many athletes suffer from a weak core which causes their body to arch, pike or both, completely missing the vital handstand position. This creates a loss of power and control limiting further progressions.

The main causes of athletes flexing at the hips is they don't squeeze their glutes long enough and they have poor core strength. Flexing the hips to complete a rotation is a way to compensate for a lack of power. This usually happens after over-arching in the initial phase of the tumble due to the same issue: a weak core. Using imagery to prompt their imagination, you can help them understand by saying something like "willow trees should not be allowed to tumble, you need to go back and learn how to a solid oak."

Core stability and strength training is very helpful, as well as breaking down a skill into three parts: the entry, the middle, and the landing (or end). Look for the point when an athlete begins to pike, then to devise a specific drill that focuses on the small movement they need to correct.

Tumbling is crooked: This is one of the easiest problems to see but one of the most difficult to fix. When in a running pass, concentrate on the athlete's roundoff and look for the feet and hands to be in alignment. It is important to slow the skill down to help an athlete find success. In standing passes, assess the athlete's strength and flexibility on the left and right side of their body, looking for imbalances in arm strength and mobility in the hamstring, wrist, and shoulder. Additionally, athletes may unconsciously turn their body away from current or past pain or to compensate for an imbalance. Addressing this with targeted strength, stretching and mobility training will usually be enough to solve the problem. Then, break the skill down slowly to help the muscles memorise the correct pathway before reintroducing the whole skill.

Tumbling on heels: When athletes tumble flat-footed or on their heels it is a sign that they are either unaware, have poor ankle strength/ mobility or weakness in their calves. You can test ankle mobility by having the athlete get into a low squat position (with their backside touching their heels, knees over their toes) and then rise to their toes, all while staying balanced. Performing a basic tumble in a controlled environment focusing on extension through the toes will also help to resolve this issue. Finally, adding strength and flexibility training for the ankles and calves will greatly improve an athlete's ability to tumble on their toes.

Landing short (needing more rotation): Most athletes land short in their tumbling when they are not rotating correctly. Increasing the athlete's awareness of their body shape (e.g. hollow or tuck) helps tremendously. Additionally, athletes can working on exercises that focus on the lower abdominals and increase the rotation speed.

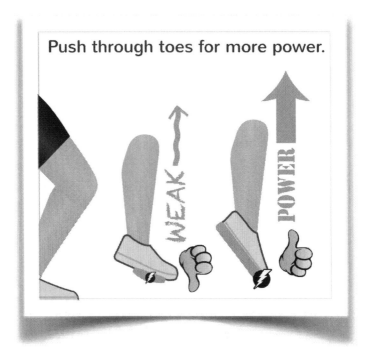

Tumbling is low: There are many reasons an athlete's tumbling is low. It could be due to a technical issue with body alignment, but it could also be a strength issue. It is recommended to mix plyometric exercises, strength, and drills to help an athlete maximise body awareness. Begin looking at the basics to see if the body shape is correct and if their hand-to-foot timing is correct.

Lethargic or slow tumbling: This is a very common problem in cheerleading today. Many athletes enjoy the comforts of trampolines and tumble tracks to help them learn new skills. However, when they transfer these skills to a harder surface (for example, a sprung floor to a dead floor, or a trampoline to a cheer floor), they either do not know they need to increase their speed and power or they do not have the power necessary to perform the skill on that harder surface. This is the equivalent of preparing for a go-cart race in a Ferrari.

Of course, using a trampoline and a tumble track is a great way to get a feel for the skill and start the progression process, but plyometrics and tumbling drills should be trained on the same surface of where the skill is to be performed. The three most common problem areas here are the glutes, hamstrings, core and shoulder strength.

MOTIONS & ENERGY

Arm motions are the original foundation of cheerleading. They are the element which makes it so iconically sharp and unique. Arm motions are present not only in motion and dance sequences but also for skills (jumps, stunting, and sometimes tumbling) which makes them a vital technique of our sport. Uniforms are even designed to accentuate the artistry of team motions. Even though motions are still present in some skills, all-star cheerleading has moved away from motion technique choreography almost completely.

It's understandable that some forms of competitive cheerleading have naturally evolved from traditional cheer, however it is also one of the reasons why newer athletes struggle with comprehending more difficult skills. By skipping motion technique training we are depriving athletes' development of the body awareness, symmetry and isometric training that are the foundations of our sport. This is a problem, specifically in countries where cheerleading is emerging, because athletes don't progress from school cheerleading or gymnastics. They jump straight into all-star training and their bodies are just not prepared for it.

If we concern ourselves with building better athletes but ignore motion technique training, we are missing the entire premise of our sport. It is like asking a gymnast to tumble without training a handstand; teaching a baby how to run without walking first. Among other factors, this is why INTENSITY workouts feature strong use of motions and why the original Cheerobics® Fitness workout was created in the first place: to build a strong cheerleading foundation with solid cheer technique and isometric training (the poms were added for the fun factor).

Then there are those that like me, the purists, suffer from nostalgia and enjoy the mechanical precision of the 'UCA style' of cheer which is more connected to our roots. I wish that all-star cheer found a way to make original techniques and styling relevant rather than moving so far away from it, the style can barely be recognised as being under the same umbrella. If you fall under this category, if you coach a college, school or sideline team or you simply want to see what 'UCA Style' cheerleading technique should look like, I highly recommend finding 'Rochester Cheer state finals' (best videos circa 2008 and 2009). That level of precision in cheer, tumble and stunting is something I hope will make a comeback in some shape or form. Who knows what all-star cheerleading will look like in years, but if you're the type of coach that wants to train athletes via the *Body Before Skill* method, the technique of motions and isometrics are drilled before anything else.

MOTION TECHNIQUE

Arms are generally straight and tight (but elbows not locked), hands in either fists or blades. All moves should be performed sharply, imagining hitting a brick wall in the air. Wrists should not be bent or 'broken.' Thumbs should be on the outside of the fists. The spiral shapes (aka cinnamon rolls) which are formed with the hand always face forward unless they are in 'touchdown' motion.

There are 5 words beginning with the letter P which are crucial to proper motion technique:

> ‣ **Punch:** Fists/punches go first. Punch the air so hard you see it move! Squeeze the fists.

> ‣ **Power:** All motions should be executed with plenty of power. This is achieved by squeezing fists and contracting arm muscles isometrically. Keep arm positions locked even if an outside force is attempting to move it.

> ‣ **Pathway:** This describes moving the motion from point A to point B in the most direct way, punching first, without breaking or swinging the motion. To avoid swinging, learn to block at

the end of the movement, as if it were hitting a brick wall. This is more easily achieved by squeezing the fists.

‣ **Position:** Arms should always be slightly in front of the shoulders even with a side motion. Fists should always be in the field of vision. To test if the position is right, ask participants to hold a High V or a T looking straight ahead: they should be able to see their fists in their field of vision looking straight ahead.

‣ **Posture:** Hips square, core engaged, legs strong without fully locking out the knees (to avoid stress on the joints), shoulders down and relaxed, chest out, head up, attempting to elongate the body towards the sky as much as possible.

MOTION TECHNIQUE ISSUES & FIXES

Identifying problems in motion technique is fairly simple, as they can be classified by the lack in one or more of the 5 P's.

It's ideal to correct arm motions with individual feedback to each athlete and with good demonstration of the technique you want to see. Repetition is key to achieve solid motion technique. Pay attention to each athlete in order to get to team uniformity. Common mistakes are:

‣ **Clap -** *Issue:* Elbows flapping out. *Instruction:* Squeeze the elbows in towards the body and keep the clap above the chest.

‣ **High-V -** *Issue:* Shoulders up to ears or arms too wide. *Instruction:* Shoulders should be relaxed down; try rolling them back. Arms should be forward and up, forming a 90-degree 'V' shape.

‣ **Low-V -** *Issue:* Low V is too narrow and close to the body. *Instruction:* The Low V should be slightly in front and an exact inversion of the High V. A good way to check this is by doing a diagonal and seeing if the line between the high and low arm are symmetrical.

▸ **T -** *Issue:* Arms behind the line of the shoulders. *Instruction:* Remind that the T should be slightly in front and arms punched into position.

▸ **Touchdown -** *Issue:* Arms too wide and bent in more of a 'U' position. *Instruction:* Keep the inside of the arms touching the sides of the head, squeezing into the ear, pulling up and straight.

▸ **Broken T or Half T -** *Issue:* Fists are almost touching or elbows are low. *Instruction:* From a perfect T position, keep upper arms completely still, fold at the elbow and bring the fists to the chest. Arms should be straight and strong and fists just below the shoulder.

▸ **Daggers -** *Issue:* Fists almost touching, elbows out. *Instruction:* Squeeze elbows in, imagining holding daggers pointing to the front, with the handle resting on the shoulders.

ENERGY & PERFORMANCE

Strong energy is necessary to a cheer performance but should only be addressed after timing and precision have been drilled. The energy is the 'finishing coat' and should serve to reinforce (not make up for) good timing and precision. It can only be applied once the team has the technical foundation and has learned the choreography.

Energy comes across in many ways, so sometimes saying 'MORE ENERGY' is ineffective in getting the results you are looking for. Athletes need to understand the full extent of the desired result. Some good instructions to improve energy levels are:

▸ Show how much you are enjoying performing: **show off** to your audience.

▸ Fight for the spotlight. You're a team, but on the mat you should aim to be noticed individually for having the best energy and technique, no matter if you're front, centre or in the back line. Do this, of course, while still being completely uniform with the rest of the team.

‣ *Control* your movements - make sure that if you have lots of energy you don't lose your good technique.

‣ Always perform as if it were your last time and it's your farewell performance. You never know what happens tomorrow, so perform as if you'll never get a chance to do it again.

‣ Always *perform* for 1st place. Other teams may have the upper hand with technical ability and skills but you'll be surprised what a good dose of energy can do to the overall enjoyment of a performance. Whatever your skill or level, everyone in the team needs to perform for 1st place.

‣ Smile with your eyes. They are the windows to your soul, and a fake smile won't fool anyone. Joy comes from within, and if your eyes sparkle with pride and joy, the rest of your body will follow.

FIXING ENERGY ISSUES

‣ **Low self-esteem:** Some people move with little energy because they are afraid to fail. They think that if they don't try too hard they can't make a fool of themselves. This may be a bigger issue than you're able to deal with in training but you can play your part to ensure that everyone feels safe and supported. Help them understand that high energy will *always* come across better than low. If anything, low energy is drawing more attention to them, but not the good kind.

‣ **High energy, swinging arms:** The energy is there but they need to focus more on CONTROLLING their movements - isolating, engaging, punching and showing off their technique when performing. Try telling them that energy isn't just what you put on top of motion technique, it's what you put *in* to motion technique.

‣ **High energy, blank face:** These cheerleaders have naturally high energy when performing but may forget to smile or perform because they are concentrating. They are not used to thinking of their faces as part of the overall performance. Encourage work on the facial expression of the whole team at every stage of the practice so that it becomes second nature and trigger facial muscle memory whenever they are performing. Music lyrics can help with this and make everyone feel more engaged.

▸ **Big smiles, low energy:** This is what we call 'fake energy,' a mask trying to make up what's really lacking. These cheerleaders need to know they can't just rely on their facial expressions to provide the energy. Focus on the punch, power and hitting the counts.

7
IMPLEMENTING CONDITIONING

The most frequent comment we hear from coaches when approaching the subject of implementing a structured fitness plan is "we would love to do more but we just don't have the time." Ask yourself:

- What happens in the first 10 minutes of practice?
- How many minutes of break are we taking in between full outs or long reps?
- What percentage of time is spent repeating stunts that just won't go up?
- How many times do we have to stop practice because of a small accident or injury?
- Out of the total amount of hours spent in the gym, what percentage of this time is *fully* being utilised?

The answers will differ from team to team, but the common denominator will always be this: time management is always an issue. People will get hurt/need to breathe/warm up/repeat the stunt, etc. Now, imagine a scenario where the first 10 minutes of your training session will help minimise:

- The time of rest in between full outs
- The time wasted due to small and larger injuries
- The amount of time it takes athletes to hit the skill
- The amount of time that athletes can get lost in chatter

When creating the INTENSITY™ method, the first concern was to create a program that would help coaches improve time management and ensure that conditioning would help structure, not conflict with, a training session. As a result, coaches can see that conditioning is not only essential to improving team strength, it is also their best asset when it comes to time management and making the most of practice.

The second aspect of creating the INTENSITY™ method was to create a series of exercises that would develop the '360 Athlete,' not just train for aesthetics. Just like other sports-specific conditioning, the goal for cheerleading is to develop drills with skill specificity to help athletes use their bodies as a whole. When creating workouts that are skill-specific, the skill itself is dissected and broken down into bite-sized sequences that can be used at drills. This can be done by examining the skill's:

- Biomechanics
- Kinetic chain movement patterns
- Muscle contractions and sequencing
- Speed and tempo
- Joint angles

The guidelines set out in this chapter form the basis of the INTENSITY™ method which was designed to put the *Body Before Skill* philosophy into practice. I happily share the foundations and principles in the hope that they will be useful for teams around the world. Of course, it might be challenging for coaches to come up with and implement the actual workouts without necessary qualifications or background in fitness. To assist, I invite any coaches out there who would like guidance and structure when implementing fitness activities to qualify through the INTENSITY™ Coach Certification. More details on this can be found at the end of this book in the *appendix* section.

IMPLEMENTING A WORKOUT

When implementing conditioning, it's not as simple as asking athletes to do X amount of pushups and run for Y amounts of laps around the gym. By now, hopefully you understand that implementing an effective conditioning plan needs thought, purpose and a specific design. We need to take into consideration

- when is the conditioning taking place in the season?
- what are we asking them to do before and after the conditioning?
- what are we asking them to do tomorrow?
- how many repetitions are we asking them to complete?
- what is the specific goal for this exercise?
- what area of the 360 athlete are we training?
- is our workout balanced overall?
- have we split our groups by ability and given enough progression options to our athletes?

Depending on the answers to the questions above, there are a number of exercises and training methods that we can use. To create a balanced workout we need to think of sets, speed, repetitions, recovery times and we need to create a balance between training all aspects of the 360 athlete without compromising their muscle, bone and joint integrity, or overall health. Individual exercises can be categorised into:

▸ **Low impact** - an exercise that keeps one foot on the ground at all times (such as marching or walking). Less challenging to the cardiovascular system but kinder on the joints.

▸ **High impact** - a movement that requires both feet to leave the floor at the same time (eg a jump or a hop). More challenging to the cardiovascular system but puts more stress on the joints.

▸ **Stationary** - the movement stays on the spot and the momentum is always vertical. It is space efficient and the leg muscles generally move in an up-down sequence.

▸ **Traveling** - the movement travels from side to side, front to back or on a multidirectional path and challenges the joints and muscles in a more varied way while relieving stress of the joints.

▸ **Calisthenic** - the movement uses body weight to create resistance (by being on the floor, on one leg, etc).

▸ **Concentric** - exercises that require the primary muscles to shorten to create movement (for example the upward phase of a squat).

▸ **Eccentric** - exercises that require the primary muscles to shorten to create movement (for example the downward phase of a squat).

▸ **Isometric** - exercises that require the muscles to contract without moving (for example motion drills, planks or headstands).

▸ **Partner work** - an exercise that requires a partner, both can be doing the same movement or they can be alternating turns.

▸ **Group work** - exercises that require three or more individuals, or even a full team, to complete the exercises.

▸ **Weights** - exercises requiring an external weight or apparatus to complete the workout.

▸ **Plyometric** - exercises that require short bursts of high energy to achieve maximum power (such as jumping on and off a high block).

‣ **Mobility** - exercises that target the connective tissue rather than the muscles, to develop better joint integrity and enhance performance potential.

‣ **Explosive strength** - training the maximum force development of a type of muscle contraction. Movement concentrates on increasing speed between maximum and minimum range of motion in the shortest amount of time possible, in rapid sequence.

‣ **Stability** - exercises that require movements to be slow and controlled to develop strength, body control and resistance (slow pushup declining to plank position).

‣ **Muscle sequencing** - exercises that drill the specific muscle memory that is required for a skill (such as cradle snaps).

‣ **Optimal surplus** - extending the usual range of motion required for a skill, training joints to have more freedom of movement and resistance (eg rotating planks).

‣ **Precision** - exercises performed to a specific timing using counts or music to increase execution and range of motion hitting specific positions on specific counts (eg training jumps).

‣ **Timed** - exercises performed within a specified duration where the goal is to maintain execution over a period of time.

‣ **To maximum speed** - exercises done to the athlete's maximum speed where the goal is to reach the maximum range of motion or amounts of repetitions within time constraints (eg how many pushups can you do in one minute).

These are some but not all of types of training exercises that can be useful to cheerleading conditioning. However, they are all relevant to different areas of training and it is important that athletes get to experience all of these aspects of cheerleading skill development. The following sections discuss how conditioning should be implemented.

PRE-SEASON CONDITIONING

The pre-season is the best time to implement conditioning standards to the team. After an adequate restoration period post competition season (which is necessary in every sport), using the summer break is a great way to build the foundation for the *Body Before Skill* concept for the new season. In cheerleading, the pre-season is usually made up of four phases (this may vary from country to country).

> ‣ **Tryouts & team placement:** At this time, athletes try to achieve the highest possible skill in order to place on their desired team. This is a great time to test the fitness level of athletes in addition to their cheer skills. Those with higher fitness levels are less likely to get injured and they will be able to cope with the pace of the team. Athletes with poor fitness might fall behind or suffer from injuries due to a deficient body. This can be a frustration to the athletes, coaches and the team as a whole, so it's important that team placement is not just based on skill but also on fitness.
>
> ‣ **Camp:** At camp, athletes usually learn the new skills that they will use for the rest of the year. Fitness levels may fall behind the technique level, making the skill more time consuming to develop. Remember, athletes have just gone through an extended rest and recovery period before the camp. It could also be caused by the effort required to perform the new skills exceeds their body's potential at this time. A level of difficulty that is too high may be the cause of injury or frustration, so it's best to focus on building solid technique until the athlete is ready for the next step. Around this time, it's also a good idea to hold a separate clinic to teach the warmup and conditioning exercises that will be used until regionals. If you do not have a fitness professional on the team or you would like to get external help, the INTENSITY™ Coach network can be useful. You may also want to consider getting a staff member on your team certified to get the full benefits of the INTENSITY™ program in-house.

‣ **Choreography:** Athletes learn how to incorporate skills into the routine; the mind has to cope with processing and remembering a lot of new information which is regularly changed. Athletes will use less energy during this time than the rest of the season because there is a lot of waiting around and piecing sections together. This time can be used wisely to push their strength and cardiovascular fitness to the limit, giving them a head start to the season. Using circuits or stations will help give structure to the choreography clinic so that all athletes are making the most of this time, even if they are not all needed together on the mat.

‣ **Skill building:** During the end of the pre-season, the team usually focuses on enhancing skill difficulty in order to score the highest possible range. This can lead to frustration when the team is growing tired and the skill requirements exceed their physical ability. This is why it is crucial to have a solid, well-structured ten minute warm up that combines skill-specificity to drill correct muscle sequencing and push cardiovascular fitness so that athletes peak at the end of the season. We also need to build a warmup that will develop these areas without losing the power and stability during the skills portion of the training session.

IN-SEASON CONDITIONING

Implementing in-season conditioning can be a challenge both in terms of time management and also maximising performance at training and competition. The season usually consists of:

- **Building full out routines:** Cheerleaders put together all the learned skills and choreography. This can create a shock to the body. At this time, cheerleaders will start to reach their peak effort, but the shock of these full outs can be minimised with cardiovascular training through the season. Teams should prioritise joint stability and physical stress management.

- **Regionals:** Routines are repeated but skills may not always be consistent. There is an increase in training time and forcing inconsistent skills can increase the risk of injury. Teams should focus on exercises that harness strength but don't tire the muscles excessively. Plan plenty of stability exercises and body recovery sessions.

- **Routine and skill adjustments:** After a competition, teams will re-adjust their routines based on scoresheet feedback to get a higher score in the next competition of the season. As a result, athletes are required to push their level of skill and effort even further. It's a good idea to change the conditioning / warm up and step up the physical challenge. Holding another small clinic to learn a new conditioning routine, progressive adaptations and team bonding is one way to prepare to meet the end of season demands.

- **Final competition:** Practice times around the final competition of the season go through the roof, and at the same time, bodies become weaker with over use so risk of injuries are at their peak. This is a time to focus on exercises that harness strength but don't tire the muscles excessively. Include plenty of joint stability exercises and body recovery sessions.

Conditioning during the season should mainly take place outside of cheer training so that power, explosiveness and joint stability is not compromised. There are four ways in which conditioning can be seamlessly added to an athlete's schedule:

‣ Including cardiovascular fitness in the first 10 minutes of warmup to push VO2 max levels and increase heart rate consistently.

‣ Using conditioning 'blitzes' during down time in training sessions.

‣ Attending the gym or doing home workouts on one or two days outside of training (note: flexibility training should be done daily, whereas strength, power and cardiovascular training can be done bi-weekly to see sufficient progress).

‣ Running a separate but compulsory skill-specific conditioning class (which is something that is required in most sports, especially in gymnastics, ice skating, or other olympic sports but is not yet the norm within our industry).

CONDITIONING IN WARMUP

The warm up section of cheerleading training is usually the one that is most overlooked and where time is not used at its best. The first 15 minutes of training are essential to help you make the most of the training session (i.e. set the tone, build the strength, stamina and endurance for the rest of the season). When executed correctly, a good warm up will:

‣ Prepare all joints through mobility, pulse raising and stretching exercises.

‣ Prepare the body for the main activity, enhance performance and reduce the risk of injury.

- Promote the release of synovial fluid into the joints to warm up the tendons, muscles and ligaments surrounding the joints to ensure that they are lubricated properly.

- Increase the heart rate, promoting the blood flow to the muscles and making the body warmer.

- Activate the brain to make the body more efficient and responsive to training.

- Build endurance to perform full outs and reduce effort during training.

- Train athletes to use music and hit counts on the beat.

- Build muscle memory with correct techniques through targeted drills.

An effective warm up uses a combination of skill-specific drills that are designed to develop appropriate muscle sequencing, technique and enhance the natural mechanics of the athlete's body. During this time:

- Athletes need to maintain a constant intensity and mild state of breathlessness: enough for people to be able to say a few words without difficulty, but not so whole sentences can be spoken in sequence.

- The coach needs to emphasise the need to control the movement: core, legs, feet, arms. They should be able to demonstrate visually and use appropriate cueing/encouragement techniques.

- The warm up sequence should aim for a 70-80% maximum heart rate, so it is a good idea to test your warm up routine in advance to check the level of intensity (it may be worth using an HR monitor on a few volunteers to test the routine effectively).

- At the end of the warm up, the coach needs to ensure the group maintains some movement for two minutes before stopping completely, to avoid blood pooling. This is when there is too much blood being pumped into the heart which cannot be pumped out rapidly enough once you stop the intense exercise.

‣ Check for signs if the intensity of the warm up is too high. This includes dizziness, loss of coordination, breathing difficulties, tightness in the chest and other pains. If these signs should manifest themselves, lower the intensity immediately, check the ventilation of the room or stop the workout if necessary.

During the months of competition, the demands of training vastly change so the schedule also needs to change with it. It would be counterproductive for athletes to get overly fatigued just before training a full out, as this would compromise the execution and the joint stability. Building strength, endurance and VO2 max is something that needs to be built at the start of the season and in-between competitions but not in the few weeks before and certainly not right before a gruelling session of full outs. When the team approaches this stage of the season, a milder version of the warmup will be a better option.

CONDITIONING DURING CHEER TRAINING

Whilst the warm up needs to drill muscle memory, stamina, endurance, lower body power and improve cardiovascular fitness, there are some other areas that need to be addressed. They are strength, arm power, core strength and progressive overload. For example, if athletes train at home using INTENSITY™ workouts or attend additional conditioning classes, they will be able to train alongside their regular cheer training, an ideal scenario. This is not always likely, and therefore, regular training will ideally include progressive overload principles.

Adding an entire section of strength and power training during a cheer practice is not always realistic due to time constraints. It would also not be beneficial to the athletes. Unnecessary muscle fatigue caused by conditioning during training is likely to weaken the joints and reduce the muscle power for when athletes need it the most: to train and develop their cheer skills.

During training sessions the INTENSITY™ method uses a similar training style that they use in the military and SEALS training: conditioning blitzes at unexpected moments. They perform a quick series of conditioning exercises (such as 12 pushups, for example) at the coach's whim (usually just after having performed a routine section or other skills). This method is used to:

> ‣ Add the element of surprise so athletes are not anticipating the strength training.

> ‣ Get athletes to pull out strength and power at their weakest, which will be beneficial when performing full outs.

> ‣ Make good use of time by only using exercises that athletes know the names of and that they are familiar with will reduce conditioning time as you won't need to be explaining it.

> ‣ Give water breaks after the blitzes, not before. A typical order of sequence would be: stunt sequence, surprise blitz, water break.

This type of training has two effects:

> ‣ **Psychologically:** Athletes don't have the time to think about what's coming. It's short, so they can put more effort into it. They exceed their own expectations by pushing through their limits.

> ‣ **Physically:** The body gains strength by pushing beyond its current threshold using the progressive overload method. However, skill execution is not compromised because conditioning blitzes are basic exercises with short duration and are scheduled at a low frequency, leaving the body enough time to recover.

CONDITIONING IN THE COOL DOWN

The last five minutes of a cheer training session should be dedicated to increasing the long-term flexibility of the athletes, lowering the heart rate back to normal and preventing DOMS (Delayed Onset Muscle Soreness). Not stretching at the end of the session could completely reverse any flexibility progress and cause injury/soreness in the following days. Stretching at the end of a session is not a question of time; it is a necessity and should always be supervised if possible. To encourage stretching at the end of a session, use a cool-down track and have coaches lead or help athletes with particular flexibility issues.

The exercises performed in this section should be developmental stretches using dynamic, static or PNF techniques. These stretches are designed to lengthen the muscles back to their pre-workout state and slightly beyond, increasing long-term flexibility. This will be achieved by holding the stretch through a slight tension, releasing and then pushing further into the stretch. This can be further achieved with a good breathing technique led by the coaches.

CONDITIONING BETWEEN TRAINING

Offering a regular conditioning class or doing home workouts in-between training is really the best way to develop the conditioning of your athletes. This way, their strengthening, flexibility, speed, power and all other athletic elements can be trained at their best by pushing themselves on days where they don't have to conserve their energies and joint integrity for skills.

The reason we created INTENSITY™ home workouts for teams and the class formats was to offer a solution tailored to cheerleading muscle sequencing and our specific conditioning needs. In addition, the pre-choreographed routines and class formats were designed for athletes to follow at their own level individually at home or in large groups. It was made so all ages and ability levels could train together, offering a time and space-efficient way for athletes to train at the same time. It also gives opportunities for parents and friends who want to take part in a fitness class. We've also seen some gyms introduce what we call "PARENTENSITY" classes. Isn't that awesome and such a bright prospect for the future? How great would it be for cheer gyms to become a centre for anyone to get involved no matter what age, level or if they are fit to compete? Without considering the fundraising benefits that this can bring to the gym too.

Regardless if you're using INTENSITY™ or another form of fitness, these activities can be a positive bonding experience and a way to involve the community. It also provides an excellent way for teams to have an ongoing fundraising activity which provides excellent benefits all year round. For more details about implementing this into your cheer community, see the appendix.

COMPETITION SEASON MAINTENANCE

We all know that injury rates peak around competition times due to increased stress and hours of training. One aspect we don't take into account, however, is that even though athletes have been conditioned and are able to perform a full cheer routine, they often lack the preparation to face a week of intense training leading up to competition. The paradox is similar to asking a sprinter to perform a marathon the day before their 1000-metre race without even having done any long-distance training.

The physical demands of a cheerleading routine are comparable to a 1000-metre race or a boxing match: they all require a blend of aerobic and anaerobic exercise with bursts of effort that require both power and strength. The week of competition, however, athletes are required to increase their training time to double, triple or even more, but their bodies are simply not prepared for this. If competitive cheer training is equivalent to sprinting, competitive cheerleaders have to sustain the 'marathon' conditions of 'peak week' before competition which often comes at a price.

This hectic training schedule and physical demand can be confusing for athlete's bodies when:

- **Athletes are poorly trained to increase their VO2max** - The ability of their bodies to utilise oxygen efficiently during aerobic respiration is essential to sustain weekends of 8+ hours of competitions and practice. This requires gradual and consistent training, which will facilitate an easier and safer transition from 2 hour practices to 4+ hour cheer marathons.

- **Athlete's muscles are not trained for endurance** - Cheer athletes predominantly have fast-twitch muscles (for short-term, explosive movement that thrive in anaerobic conditions) as opposed to slow-twitch muscles (for long-term endurance exercise that requires oxygen). Once they arrive at the weekend of competition, their fast-twitch muscles are not suited to the amount of prolonged stress which they will undergo.

- **Athletes are not used to having their heart rate above 80% for more than 30 seconds at a time** - the sudden strain can cause dizziness, hyperventilation and heatstroke as their bodies reach higher temperatures than usual.

- **DOMS and Lactic Acid** - Long training on weekends will build up more lactic acid and cause delayed onset muscle soreness (DOMS). Athletes will reach a blood-lactic threshold which is beyond their usual limits. They simply cannot meet the energy demands of training during the following days until the lactic acid has fully broken down and the muscles have fully recovered. DOMS will also cause tenderness and discomfort in the muscles, which will make it harder for athletes to perform with proper technique, inducing injury.

- **Repeated impact and strain on the joints** - Repeated impact will cause the joints to be weaker when performing for longer. Research published by the *Journal of Orthopaedic & Sports Physical Therapy* suggests that as little as 2 hours of intense cheer practice may be too much for the joints to sustain their functions safely.

Endurance training for competition weekend needs to be planned in advance: it starts in the off-season and gradually increases for competition training. The last few weeks before the competition are not a good time to focus on building strength, but are better suited to help athletes:

- Be mentally prepared to take the floor
- Reduce the risk of getting injured
- Know how much energy they need on the day
- Improve their level of execution
- Understand the risk of deductions
- Build morale, along with parents and coaches

The competition season should focus on:

‣ **Memory:** Knowledge of the routine should be solid, but athletes need to be adaptable to any changes if coaches need to add difficulty or simplify the routine. Athletes can help mental stress by being adaptable to change, visualising their routine regularly in order to cement those counts in their procedural memory.

‣ **Skill:** By now, athletes should know *what* they are doing but they need to focus on the *how*. If necessary, take a video of the skill to share and discuss. Are they performing to their absolute best and fully executing the technique you've asked them to? Athletes can watch videos of their favourite teams to inspire them to add technical performance to their execution.

‣ **Endurance:** Including a few short bursts of endurance training outside of cheer practice (5-10 minutes of INTENSITY™ training for example, 3-5 times a week) will keep athletes conditioned for the cardiovascular and stamina spikes they will experience closer to the weekend of competition.

‣ **Flexibility:** If needed, flexibility can be improved in a short space of time, as long as it's done on a daily basis and counteracted with stability training so that it does not negatively affect joint integrity. Athletes should work on overall body flexibility, not just for skills, so that fixator and antagonist muscles are also stretched. Athletes should be reminded that developmental flexibility should be worked on at the end of the day or training session and never before stunting, tumbling or jumps.

‣ **Stability:** Because the exposures to cheerleading activities increase in the weeks before a competition, there are more opportunities for joint stability to become compromised and injury to occur. Rest, recovery and focusing on stability exercises should be prioritised over power or strength development.

‣ **Nutrition:** What athletes eat around competition time will have a direct impact on their amount of energy. This affects both the level of execution and injury risk. Carb loading during the 48-hours prior to the competition is a proven way to reach peak athletic performance, but this does not include cotton candy and popcorn! For a more in-depth guide of what you should be eating during competition month and all season long, I highly recommend reading and using the tips mentioned in *The Cheer Diet* by coach Sahil M. for a good understanding.

- **Hydration:** Athletes should drink plenty of water outside of training. Sports drinks can be a good idea as long as they are not laden with sugar. Coconut water is a great source of electrolytes. Athletes should try to avoid drinking lots before or during training because it can result in loss of power.

- **Mental:** Ensuring athletes are fully confident with the required skills under pressure will be crucial to their performance. It's easy to perform a skill in isolation and a whole lot different when doing it in a full out routine.

- **Care:** Getting plenty of sleep and trying to avoid all digital devices one hour before falling asleep can be highly beneficial, especially around competition. Instead, athletes should spend this time listening to music, reading and proactively recovering (eg. bathing with Epsom salts which will nurse sore muscles into recovery). At night, the room should be nice and dark and at a good, cool temperature (never cold or stuffy).

- **Jet lag:** If required, adapting to a new time zone as soon as the team steps onto the plane can be very useful. The simple trick is to stay awake during daytime and sleep if it's night at your final location. The best way to prevent jet lag is by tricking your body clock by not thinking about what time it is back home, adapting to the new time zone. Mind over matter can be of great help here.

- **Tapering:** Tapering is the concept of rest or reduced training before a race or competition. It is commonly used as a peak performance method in a number of sports, allowing the body to restore muscle tissue to optimum condition when it matters the most. The downside of tapering in cheerleading is that teams warm up and have trainings on the competition weekend. These trainings can be a good way of refreshing, fixing any last-minute issues, getting used to new conditions and cleaning up the routine. Complete rest for 48 hours before a competition is not realistic, but we need to significantly reduce the intensity levels we put on our athletes the days before the competition.

‣ **Acclimatisation:** Athletes may not be used to the humidity or heat if competing in a new location. Imagine a northern European team leaving wintery conditions and arriving in hot and humid Florida ready for Worlds! Training and performing in a new climate might cause athletes to overheat and fatigue rapidly, so this needs to be taken into consideration if planning long training sessions on location.

‣ **Motivation:** A number of mental preparation techniques can be used to maximise the attitude athletes will take onto the mat. Refreshing the chapter on *"A Winning Attitude"* will be of use alongside writing a short affirmation or pep talk for the team and for individual athletes.

FITNESS PROGRESSIONS

Understanding the different fitness levels of your athletes is an important aspect of health and safety which will also help you to motivate and develop their skills. When introducing a new conditioning regimen, it is not necessary to split the training between teams or age groups unless their levels are significantly different. (For example, Youth 1 and Junior 2 may train together, as well as Senior 4 and Junior 5, but not Youth 1 and Senior 4). In mixed training session or open classes, coaches will find that skill levels vary and you must be flexible so that your teachings can be applicable to everyone's needs.

Variables which determine the intensity and difficulty of your workout plan need to include variables in:

- Resistance and range of motion
- Speed (rate at which the exercises are performed)
- Training method (continuous vs fartlek)
- Choreography
- Music
- Sets/rests/repetitions

The '360 athlete' principle will be entirely different from person to person. The spectrum of levels depend on age, build, athletic history and a number of other variables that were discussed in the earlier chapters of this book.

Progressions are not only necessary for safety precautions but also to develop good muscle memory. A skill repeated and drilled badly (above ability) will result in poor execution and bad habits. It may give short-term advantages (such as learning a high-scoring skill for a competition) but in the long run it can result in more severe issues such as a progression block or, even worse, injury.

There is a fine line between pushing a team so that they can progress to new skills and putting athletes at risk. Confident athletes may be more reluctant to spend time perfecting a skill before progressing and can become impatient when learning a new skill. It is important to give athletes tangible and measurable targets that they can use as a motivation tool.

The areas that require attention in regards to fitness progression are:

▸ **Cardiovascular fitness:** Beginners will be out of breath and have a higher heart rate response. Use a lower intensity and a slower speed of music. As intermediate athletes' heart rate and breathlessness will increase at a normal rate, they can be encouraged to push at full intensity and achieve a full range of motion in all exercises. Advanced athletes will have a steady heart rate and breathlessness, so you can increase the intensity, range of motion and speed of music

▸ **Flexibility:** Beginners will have a low range of motion, so use correct breathing technique to ease them gently into movement with full control. Stop if pain becomes sharp. Intermediate level athletes will see their range of motion improving, so they can ease into their stretches with correct technique and push a little further by breathing deeply with the movement. Athletes with advanced flexibility will have an almost complete range of motion. They can hold stretches for longer and use a partner or external force to help push further as long as they keep control. PNF stretching can be very effective for these athletes.

▸ **Strength:** Beginners will have low levels of strength. Lowering the number of repetitions, decreasing the load, lever and/or range of motion will encourage them to perform movements with the right technique before increasing the variables over time. When strength improves, the repetitions become easier. Once athletes reach a good level of strength they can increase the loads, repetitions, and sets and start training more aggressively with the progressive overload method.

▸ **Power:** Athletes with low levels of explosive power cannot complete a full range of motion due to slow speed. This gets confused in cheerleading as failure to reach a certain range may have nothing to do with flexibility or strength. Power is a separate ability linked to fast-twitch muscles and connective tissue. If an athlete shows low levels of power, decrease the speed of music and increase gradually every week. There should always be equal focus on the return of movement (snap down, landing, etc.). Next, there are athletes who can complete the full range of motion but their execution will be slow. Athletes need to focus on isometric contractions at the top of the movement (squeezing) on the beat. Training selective recruitment of fast-twitch muscles through plyometrics and explosive power training will be extremely beneficial. Once athletes achieve full range of motion to the beat, they can be pushed to perform beyond their range of motion.

‣ **Endurance:** Athletes at the lower end of this scale will struggle to complete a full set, so they will need to reduce the load and range of motion. Next, there are those who struggle to complete the set with good technique, so they can reduce the load but should go to full range of motion. If athletes are able to complete a full set without problems, they can now increase the load, range of motion or number of repetitions.

‣ **Coordination:** Athletes may struggle to complete an exercise because they do not understand the movement or their muscle sequencing may be off. Breaking down the movement and asking them to perform only one part until they find their rhythm is a first step, and you can also decrease the speed. Athletes who are learning the movement but cannot execute it with correct technique will need to break it down and repeat the exercise in isolation until it is fully mastered. Once the athlete can perform the exercise fully, they can comfortably increase the load, range of motion or speed. If the execution is excellent, they can be put in charge of demonstrating and assisting the teammates.

‣ **Motivation variable:** Motivation of the athlete can be a contributing factor to their performance. If they are struggling with the workout, their motivation will be low during difficult exercises with high bursts when the skill is achieved. They will need motivation and praise for their efforts using white horse coaching. As motivation increases along with the skills, they might come across hurdles. Praise and focusing on technical improvements. At the other end of the spectrum, the athlete can have high motivation but may become disinterested if they are finding the workout too easy. Add more variety and challenges or have them assist and demonstrate to the rest of the class.

‣ **Joint integrity:** Weaker joints, especially when overweight or lacking of body control, have an increased vulnerability to high impact exercises so they will need to be reduced to low impact. High impact exercises can be swapped with traveling exercises and athletes need to be given constant reminders to *control* the movement. Once the joints are stronger, you can add more high impact exercises to the workout, gradually training their optimal surplus. Higher impact exercises on the spot can be included once joint integrity is more stable. Keep the body aware and in control, but increase impact, weight or range of motion.

The methods described above should be used with care and only in the hands of a qualified fitness trainer or INTENSITY™ coach. Please ensure that if you are giving guidance to athletes or groups of people of any age, that you do so with care, adequate preparation, understanding and qualifications.

AGE ADAPTATIONS

Names for age divisions and classifications in cheerleading vary from country to country, so for the purpose of this chapter we have divided athletes into four groups: Minis (5-8yrs), Juniors (9-12yrs), Seniors (13-18yrs) and Open (18yrs+). Of course, every athlete will be different both psychologically and physically, so these groups address the majority as opposed to defining the nature of each individual athlete.

5-8 YEARS (MINIS)

Children between the ages of 5 and 8 are in the stages of development where they are fine-tuning their motor skills. They are starting to understand concepts such as rhythm, sequence and body awareness. Children at this age need constant stimulation, so activities should be varied and full of 'play' while linking action to the beats of the music.

Conditioning for Minis should be fun and stimulating.

- Fitness and coordination levels will extremely vary within this age group, so it is better to keep the groups smaller or have more coaches per team.
- Minis will have lower level of self-awareness.
- Minis attention may be volatile.
- Minis will respond well to authority and usually follow instructions.
- As with adults, personalities will vary from being very shy to very vocal, so having rules in place for speaking and responding is key.
- Shy individuals can be stimulated by being put in charge of small activities and/or asked questions out loud at training.
- Minis will lose interest if the task is too technical, difficult or long.

9-12 YEARS (JUNIORS)

Children between the ages of 9 and 12 will have developed stronger fine motor skills (such as writing and handling small objects) so they are able to deal with more difficult choreography and skills as well as keep concentration for longer periods of time. In some ways, this is the easiest of all age groups to manage. They can show some of the quickest results as they will accept their coach as a figure of authority and be more confident in experimenting with new skills. Conditioning for Juniors should have a good balance between play, skills, discipline and understanding the basics of teamwork.

- Fitness and co-ordination will vary but show significant differences from Minis. Juniors are more able to grasp the concepts of rhythm and body awareness though there will still be individual differences.

- Participants have a good sense of self-awareness, both physically within the space and personally when interacting.

- Juniors are willing to test new skills and are very enthusiastic. Ensure all activities are safe and that they understand what is required. Offer guidance when trying new skills.

- Juniors will respond to authority and usually follow instructions well.

- Some personalities will be very loud and others very shy. Continue to promote equilibrium and the rule that children raise their hand before speaking.

- Shy or disruptive individuals can be positively stimulated by being put in charge of small activities, such as counting out loud, collecting equipment etc.

- Juniors can still lose interest if the task is too technical, difficult or long.

13-18 YEARS (SENIORS)

Teenagers are more suited to cardiovascular training. Though teens start to develop the basics of overall fitness, they still have problem areas like bad posture, low confidence, a weak core and challenging authority. At this age, they still need to be stimulated in a way that keeps their attention throughout the session but they will want to be challenged as they do this.

> ‣ Fitness and coordination levels will vary greatly within the group.
>
> ‣ Increased self-awareness can result in shyness which can be an additional obstacle to building confidence and performance.
>
> ‣ The unruly nature of teenagers will make them more likely to stand up to authority.
>
> ‣ Teenagers will be very quick to make judgments, so making a firm impression at the start and being consistent with rule keeping is of great importance.
>
> ‣ Seniors will not respect a class that is too easy so keep it challenging enough.
>
> ‣ Seniors can become apathetic if a class is too challenging as they will feel like they can't succeed and may not want to try for fear of failure or through sheer laziness. Ensure that there is plenty of gratification that links to skill.

18 YEARS+ (OPEN)

Athletes over the age of 18 have a great advantage of better body awareness, having enough experience to take direction and being closer to achieving their athletic peak (as long as their body has not been injured or experienced over-training too many times). The independent nature of an Open athlete is your best asset but also comes with its frustrations and downsides. Open teams can either be extremely successful or extremely hard work. Finding a middle ground here is much less likely than in the other age groups, especially when the coaches and athletes are of similar ages. In this age bracket, the most important areas to address is are communication, setting expectations, and valuing every athlete but also making sure every athlete knows they are replaceable.

▸ Fitness and co-ordination levels should be at their peak as long as the athlete is actively training. They are also likely to be competitive, so use this to your advantage.

▸ At this age, athletes will be more confident as performers and teammates.

▸ As adults, they will all have opinions and want to be heard. Much time can be wasted through discussing, debating, and questioning. It's crucial to set expectations from the start a staff member who knows how to keep their cool and who is good at keeping discipline both on and off the training mat will be your strongest asset.

▸ Ignoring opinions and voices will cause disruption too. Ensure there is a person or a system in place for receiving feedback in a constructive manner so that it can be addressed in a way that is helpful and non-disruptive to training and team management.

▸ Adults will have expectations and demand instant gratification which comes with newly found independence. Along with all other training, you can add a few pieces of 'candy' (ie skills/stunts that can be achieved within a shorter timescale) to satisfy this need and keep them interested.

‣ It's important to have fun too, so schedule plenty of time to get creative, play games and be social as long as it's not conflicting with the rules of training.

‣ Delegation can be a strong asset, as well as giving coaching opportunities to those that prove to be team players. Giving people something to do is a great way to use their energies in a constructive way and make everyone feel like they are a valuable member of the team.

‣ Non-compliance needs to be addressed before it becomes a real problem. Keep your Open 'ecosystem' free from negativity and you will have an athletically and socially successful team of adults.

SAFETY PRECAUTIONS

CHEERLEADING RISKS & PREVENTIONS

▸ **Sprains** - *Due to: weakening of the joints due to overstretching.* Athletes that train long-term flexibility before skill training run the risk of weakening the muscle fibres and the joints. Ensure athletes are aware of difference of warm-up stretching versus long-term flexibility stretching.

▸ **Bailing on the skill** - *Due to: self-doubt.* Ensure athlete has gone through appropriate progressions and more than enough skill conditioning before executing so they are fully aware that their body is capable of performing the new skill.

▸ **Impact on hitting the floor** - *Due to: poor surface, poor spotting.* In no circumstance do we recommend training or performing on a surface that is not appropriate. In absence of mats or grass we recommend performing 1 or 2 levels below training ability, with sufficient spotting.

▸ **Ankle sprains on dismounts** - *Due to: bases not lowering flyer enough to the floor, poor control of dismount to ground.* Ensure athletes spend same amount of time drilling dismounts to floor as they do on the load. Most of these injuries happen because insufficient time has been spent drilling the dismount.

▸ **Lumbar strain** - *Due to: lordosis, poor core strength.* Athletes that have an exaggerated curvature of the lumbar spine, especially during basing, and a weak TVA (core) muscle can place additional strain on the lower back. This can be prevented by conditioning headstands and squat exercises with focus on tucking tailbone under on a regular basis.

▸ **Muscle fatigue** - *Due to: over-training.* Ensure training hours are increased gradually rather than suddenly. Athletes's bodies will not be conditioned for marathon-like circumstances unless they are trained for endurance.

▸ **Re-injury** - *Due to: training on an unhealed injury.* Ensure athlete receives as much recovery time as required before training again. Asking an athlete to train on an injury is irresponsible and detrimental to their long-term athletic career and welfare.

▸ **Injury on full outs** - *Due to: poor VO2max / muscle failure.*
Athletes need to be conditioned so that their bodies can utilise as much oxygen as possible with their heart rate at 80% - 90%. Include 5-10 min of high intensity cardio training at every training and include BLITZES.

▸ **ACL tear** - *Due to: Landing whilst still rotating and wide hip angle in women (special case).* There is a strong correlation between wide hips and ACL tears due to the strain caused by the angle of the bone going from the hip to the knee. This is most common in post-pubescent females. The knee joint bears most of the twisting force when landing a twisting and/or rotating skill. Strengthen the knee joint and pay particular attention to senior female athletes.

REDUCING INJURY RATE AT TRAINING

The risks of injury in cheerleading is imminent; however, there are a number of issues that cause this risk to rise. It is a coach's responsibility to be aware of all these physical dangers and help prevent risk.

▸ **Preparation:** Ensure all athletes are mentally and physically prepared to learn the next progression. Any insecurities can spark bailing and stress reactions during the skill which can result in an accident.

▸ **Progression and qualification:** Cheerleading injury rates are significantly higher in teams where the coach has fewer qualifications and experience. Coaches should receive training and certifications from reputable cheerleading organisations to ensure they fully understand the mechanics of the skills they are teaching. Sufficient spotting is crucial when the team is learning a new skill.

‣ **Temperature & ventilation:** The temperature of the gym should always be warm, but never so hot that athletes could suffer from heat-stroke. If the room is cold, lengthen the warm up and shorten the cool down/stretch. In this case, still stretch required muscles, but shorten the time of the stretch to avoid the muscles cooling down too rapidly at the point when you are focused on lengthening them. Open windows only if it is warmer outside, in order to avoid cold drafts which may cause muscular injuries. If the room is very warm shorten the warm up, lower the intensity of the training and encourage plenty of water breaks.

‣ **Humidity:** Humidity reduces the body's ability to evaporate sweat. The body produces sweat so that the evaporation process cools the temperature of the body to avoid heat stroke. This is especially important with exercise as the body's temperature increases. If the air already contains water vapour (high humidity), evaporation will be difficult and the body is more at risk of heat stroke. In high temperatures and humidity, allow for enough breaks between full outs and encourage even more water consumption.

‣ **Floor:** Ideally, you should be training on a sprung floor in order to minimise impact and stress to the joints. If this is not possible, minimise jumping and high impact exercises to preserve joint integrity. The surface should be clean and dry enough for participants to feel comfortable carrying out exercises on the floor. All rooms where cheer activities take place must have adequate mats placed a reasonable distance away from walls and high ceilings. When training outdoors, ensure the ground is dry and pay extra attention to progressions. If necessary take turns to spot new stunts until they are fully stable.

‣ **Attire:** Clothing should be comfortable and allow the skin to breathe. High content of spandex and wet-look clothing will cause the body to overheat and prevent ventilation. A supportive shoe with a shock-resistant sole is ideal to prevent inflammation and stress fracture of the sesamoid bones, which are located at the root of the toes, on the widest part of the foot. The ankle should equally be supported to avoid repetitive strain injuries and sprains during high-impact exercises. Shoes such as plimsolls and pumps should not be worn. All jewellery should be removed for cheer activities to reduce the risk of catching or scratching.

‣ **Nutrition:** Setting an example for our athletes and helping to guide the parents in making better choices for their children are important. The book *The Cheer Diet* by Coach Sahil M. provides excellent guidance for those who wish to explore the subject in more depth.

‣ **Psychology:** Athletes who are suffering from a mental block or simple fear are more likely to be injured when training the skill as they might bail/make preventable mistakes. *UnBlocked: The Walls Come Tumbling Down* by Jeff Benson is a must read for all athletes, parents and coaches.

‣ **Energy loss:** When the body goes into metabolic rate (burns fat) we lose approximately 30% of our energy. For sports training, fat loss during a training session is not desirable because it significantly inhibits performance (if the athlete wishes to decrease their body fat percentage this should be done outside of training). To avoid this, athletes should eat from a healthy source of carbohydrates (such as a pasta with a healthy sauce, oats or sweet potatoes) a few hours before training.

‣ **Overtraining:** Overtraining is a big problem in cheerleading because it does not always follow consistent methods of progressive overload or planning for peak performance in mind.

COMPETITION SEASON RISKS & PREVENTION

The week of competition, risk of injury is at its highest rate of the season. How much of this is preventable? And why exactly is there such a high concentration of injury at a time when athletes should be at their peak? Stress, fatigue and higher probability caused by the total number of skill repetitions performed are the obvious culprits. If we dig a little deeper, we can identify 8 main causes for the increased injury rate:

1. **Longer training hours:** On average, athletes triple their weekly training time before competition, increasing the number of skills executed within a certain time frame, thus increasing the probability rate of injury during that week.

2. **Poor cardiovascular training:** Athletes' are not used to marathon-like training schedules. This is a weakness that will affect how oxygen is distributed around the body, causing muscle failure. It is not something they can mentally overcome - they have to be physically trained to manage it.

3. **Body composition:** Muscle fibres are trained for short bursts of activity, not for long sessions which combine aerobic and anaerobic (lactic) training. This can also cause muscle failure (see section on *Speed & Power* and *Muscle Anatomy*).

4. **Delayed Onset Muscle Soreness (DOMS) and lactic acid:** Long training sessions can cause DOMS and the muscle lactic-blood threshold exceeding its usual capabilities. Athletes will not be able to meet the energy demands of training during the following days until the lactic acid has broken down. DOMS will also cause tenderness in the muscles and mild to severe discomfort, making it harder for athletes to perform correct technique which could induce injury.

5. **Repeated impact and strain on the joints:** This will cause joints to be weaker when performing for longer, and points 1-4 above will only aggravate this further. There is research (published by the *Journal of Orthopaedic & Sports Physical Therapy*) that suggests that even 2 hours of intense cheer practice may be too much for the joints to sustain safely.

6. **Pressure to achieve a skill:** The pressure to reach a higher score and to not let their coaches and teammates down becomes greater around competition time if the athlete hasn't achieved the progression yet. Over-training the skill with poor execution will increase the chances of injury as the body may not be physically ready to execute it consistently and safely.

7. **Poor stress management:** Getting nervous before and during competition is perfectly normal, but some athletes may find it harder to deal with than others. Some athletes also manifest physical side effects of stress (e.g. shaking, excessive sweating, nausea, faintness or an unwillingness to eat prior to competing), that could inhibit their physical performance (see section on *Mind & Focus* to explore this further).

8. **Poor nutrition:** The food that cheerleaders eat especially the week of and at competition is one of the biggest culprits of the body failing during that time. Eating poorly before and during competition is easy because of the stress, time available and choices available. If cheerleaders are serious about being considered athletes, they should follow the example of gymnasts on how they during peak times of effort. Gym owners and coaches should also take a stand in regards to what drinks and food are made available to athletes during training and at competition, given that venues are notorious for supplying junk food (which, it should be clear, is for spectators - not athletes).

SELECTION BY DESIGN

As we come to the end, hopefully you have picked up a few new ideas or looked at something you already knew but found a new spin on it. Perhaps you scanned through the pages that captured your interest the most. Maybe you went straight to the section you wanted some quick answers to. I would like to leave you with one final consideration before you take your next steps, whichever they may be. By observing the patterns within our industry in comparison to other sports (and this of course, varies from country to country as well as in different types of competitive cheerleading), we cannot help but notice the sheer volume of athletes that compete. The business of cheerleading and the cheer gym system requires that instead of turning athletes away, they are placed in a relevant group.

Everyone competes to their ability. What a wonderful concept to give equal opportunities to all participants! Dance schools, ice-skating, gymnastics, swimming, or most other sports are not built on this concept. In most cases, only the 'elite' get selected to compete. Up to 10-15 years ago, the majority of cheerleading functioned in the same way. Even though this concept has meant a great deal of positive aspects for athletes, coaches and gyms, it has also reinforced athlete progression by 'natural selection' in contrast to selection 'by design'.

The concept of natural selection can be found in evolutionary biology. It is the survival of the fittest where those with the strongest traits survive. Selection by design is an entirely different concept: instead of letting nature decide, man selects and refines the traits artificially. Similarly in cheerleading, the strongest and more naturally apt athlete will find it easier to make their way up the progression ladder. Due to the abundance of athletes to choose from, those athletes who are less prone to injury and have a superior kinaesthetic intelligence are able to move through the ranks more rapidly. Even though private tumbling classes and camps might be a great way to focus on developing an athlete's skill, by being relatively unconcerned with the physical development of the athlete we are significantly reducing the potential of building stronger teams of athletes.

In contrast, the selection by design model creates a level playing field within our teams. A chain is only as strong as its weakest link, and if we spent a little extra time ensuring they are all of equal strength the selection process would become much more interesting. We would level more appropriately and our teams as a whole would step up their potential. If we did this, we could truly build a sport based on robust foundation rather relying on creative flair and selecting from the most naturally apt.

Of course, there are many teams and cheerleading communities out there that are already implementing ideas and methods similar to those mentioned in this book. Most of the theory and technical areas we have covered are used in most other sports but are not yet used consistently throughout our industry. If you have reached this chapter thinking "that was interesting to scan, but how is it going to help me?" know this: your ability to understand and process that information will give you the same advantage as a race-car driver who is a good mechanic.

Yes, our industry has survived so far and grown without having this prior knowledge as the standard. So why make use of this now? **Imagine what can happen to our sport** if this knowledge and understanding became the standard. **Imagine what would happen if we levelled out the playing field** and helped those athletes that needed that little extra attention to step up to the same level as those who are naturally apt.

Whether we like it or not, our sport is evolving. With the international boom, we are at the start of a renaissance similar to other sports (such as rugby, baseball, snowboarding) that experienced this sort of evolution. Established olympic sports such as gymnastics have been using these techniques for decades and they've become the universal standard.

It is with the hope that you flick back through the chapters of this book until the facts have sunk in and understanding WHY rather blindly than following printed instructions before implementing them. I also hope that reading this book will inspire your curiosity to spark your journey to *Body Before Skill*. Explore. Inform. Improve. Inspire others to do the same.

"Knowledge is power. Information is liberating.
Education is the premise of progress" - Kofi Annan

8
APPENDIX

GLOSSARY

Ballistic stretches - a form of stretching with utilises an external force to push the range of motion, such as weight, bouncing, or dynamic movement with little control. This method is not recommended as it can cause injury.

Blood pooling - blood entering the heart at higher speed as a result of exercise whilst no longer being required as muscles are no longer in use.

Body fat percentage - measurement which directly calculates the body composition, a far more accurate and beneficial way than by using weight or BMI.

Calisthenic - exercises that develop physical condition through body weight without the need of any additional equipment.

Catastrophic injuries - a severe injury to the spine, spinal cord or the brain which could be life threatening.

Centre of gravity - the point which the weight of the body acts from, helping us to find stability. It is also known as the centre of mass. The lower the centre of gravity, the more stability. In stunting, the centre of gravity will shift up the line of gravity becoming the stability point of the full stunt. When rotating, the centre of gravity also becomes the centre of rotation.

Cognitive ability - brain based skills we need to carry out tasks. It is our ability to learn, remember and make use of knowledge as opposed to the actual knowledge.

Deliberate practice - the repetitive performance of intended cognitive and motor skills.

Dynamic stretching - a form of stretching that uses controlled movement and momentum to improve range of motion.

Effort - the force exerted by the body to create movement.

Explosive strength training - training using the maximum force development of a type of muscle contraction (isometric, concentric, eccentric). Requires maximum effort but a smaller number of repetitions.

Exposures - the amount of calculated times an athlete is exposed to the activity: this can include training, a competition or other types of participation (e.g. a football game or performance).

Fartlek - varied intensities of training during an activity which is typical to cheerleading training. Instead of being continuous or with intervals and peaks, fartlek is inconsistent with bouts of high intensity, low intensity rest and recovery during one session.

Fast twitch - a muscle fibre that contracts rapidly, and provides power rather than endurance. Whiter in appearance, they mainly use anaerobic respiration by tapping into stored forms of carbohydrates as a source of energy.

Fulcrum - the point on which a lever rests or is supported and on which it pivots. A fulcrum is used in callisthenics training to determine the load of resistance.

Glycemic Index - the system used to rank foods on a 1-100 scale to determine the effects on blood-sugar levels and energy release rates.

Hypertrophy - the enlargement of a muscle through an increase in size of its cells. It can be Sarcoplasmic (visual) increasing the volume of fluid in the muscle cell, or Myofibrillar (functional) increasing the proteins in the muscle.

High impact - a movement that requires both feet to leave the floor at the same time (eg a jump or a hop).

HIIT - High Intensity Interval Training consists of repeated bouts of high intensity exercise intervals mixed with low intensity exercises, allowing the heart rate to fluctuate during the workouts.

Isometric training - a type of strength training where the joint angle does not change and there are no contractions (e.g. planks).

Kinaesthetic intelligence - our body's natural ability to process movements in a skilful manner without necessarily understanding the process or conscious thought.

Kinetic chain - the reaction that happens to facilitate a specific movement. Understanding and reading the kinetic chain of a skill can help us identify how to strengthen, train and give a better mechanical advantage.

Line of gravity - an imaginary vertical line that passes through our centre of gravity down to the base of support.

Load - the mass that creates resistance against a movement. The load is dependent upon momentum, support, or lever.

Low impact - an exercise that keeps one foot on the ground at all times (such as marching or walking).

Macronutrient - a food element that is required in large amounts for the normal growth and maintenance of the body.

Mechanical advantage - When the body mechanics are used in a way that a small force can move a bigger force, requiring less effort.

Metabolic rate - the rate at which the body utilises energy, and can therefore be used as the rate to measure how quickly calories are burned with exercise or rest.

MHR - Maximum Heart Rate, i.e. the age and health related number of beats per minute of the heart when it reaches its maximum (100%). To estimate, subtract the age from 220.

Micronutrients - a food element that is required in small amounts for the normal growth and maintenance of the body.

Mindset - the established attitude held by someone. Can be categorised as fixed or growth.

Mobility - the maximum range of motion of a joint.

Natural selection - the process that describes naturally more apt or resistant athletes as they move up the level ranks of the gym's team hierarchy.

Optimal surplus - training beyond range of motion or beyond the force required so that in case of an accident or performing beyond normal conditions, the body is prepared for and more resilient against potential injury.

Perceptual motor skills - the ability to receive, interpret and respond to sensory information which results in the development of a skill.

Periodisation - the season planning of physical training, usually consisting of cycles. The goal of effective periodisation is to reach the best possible performance during the most important time of the year.

Peripheral Nervous System (PNS) - The PNS is the communication network of the body. It is made up of nerves that branch out from the brain to the and spinal cord and to all the body parts.

Physical trainability - the body's natural ability to respond to physical training. It is a range that is measured by observing an athlete's bottom line (or natural ability) and their maximum performance peak through training.

Plyometric training - a type of training designed to develop power by exerting maximum force between two contractions in short time intervals.

Procedural memory - the long-term memory associated to motor skills which is extremely difficult to reverse once achieved for a particular skill or technique.

Progressive overload: the gradual increase of training variables such as intensity, frequency, resistance, speed, fatigue levels and other external factors.

Range of motion: the measurement of the movement around a specific joint, taking into account the mechanical and neurological aspects of the joint's flexibility.

SAID principle - Specific Adaptation to Imposed Demands, i.e. the manner in which the body adapts to a specific stress/challenge. This can be used in a variety of ways to give the body a chance to adapt to a particular physical demand (eg a specific routine or skill) as long as enough time and repetitions are given.

Selection by design - the process that describes careful design and development of an athlete's skill and resistance to help them move up the level ranks of the gym's team hierarchy and to prolong their careers.

Selective recruitment - using specific drills and types of training to develop either fast-twitch or slow-twitch muscle fibres.

Skill specificity - using conditioning or drills designed to develop the SAID principle and procedural memory for a particular skill.

Slow-twitch - red muscle fibres that allow long endurance being specifically apt in using aerobic respiration.

Stretch reflex - muscle contraction in response to stretching which occurs as a natural reflex by the body to regulate the range of motion.

Tapering - the practice of reducing the exercise and effort during the few days before a competition, essential for optimal performance in the right circumstances.

Total fitness - achieving a balance of all aspects within fitness: physical, nutritional, mental, environmental, psychological, spiritual, behavioural and social.

Triple extension - describes the full extension of the three joints - hip, knee and ankle - which results in explosive power when it occurs simultaneously and with maximum force.

VO2 max - The maximum amount of oxygen that the body can make use of during exercise. It combines maximum lung capacity as well as the efficiency of our body to distribute and make use of all the available oxygen. VO2 max can generally be increased through appropriate training over time.

White horse thinking - the concept that describes using positive forms of language to instruct an action and give feedback to help visualise the desired outcome or objective.

Whole foods - a food that is consumed in its natural state or with minimum alteration, free from additives and artificial substances.

360 Athlete - symbolises the athlete who achieves the overall combination of the fitness elements required to be fully optimised for the *Body Before Skill* concept.

FURTHER READING

The Sports Gene - David Epstein , 2013 Yellow Jersey

Outliers - Malcolm Gladwell, 2008 Little, Brown and Company

The Cheer Diet - Sahil Mulla, 2015 Createspace Publishing Platform

Sports Biomechanics: The Basics- Anthony, J. Blazevich, 2007, A&C Black

UnBlocked: The Walls Come Tumbling Down - Jeff Benson, 2016 Createspace Publishing Platform

Pocket Atlas of the Moving Body - Mel Cash, 2007   Ebury Publishing

Body Maintenance and Repair - Steve Vickery and Marilyn Moffat, 1999 Holt, Henry & Company

Jumping into Plyometrics - Donald A. Chu, 1998, Human Kinetics

The Ultimate Guide to Calisthenics - Ashley Kalym, 2014, CreateSpace

8 Weeks to SEALIFT - Mark Divine, 2014 St. Martin's Press

Periodisation Training for Sports - Tudor Bompa and Carlo Buzzichelli, 2005   Human Kinetics Publishers

Return To Life - Joseph H. Pilates, 2012 Pilates Method Alliance, Incorporated; 2nd edition

INTENSITY™ FOR YOUR TEAM

The Cheerobics® INTENSITY™ programme was designed to push you to the best of your abilities and maximise what your body is capable of. It will help cheerleaders to:

- Be leaner, faster, stronger
- Develop motor skills, power, speed and endurance
- Improve resistance to performing full out routines
- Drill & perfect techniques for jump, tumble, stunt & dance
- Be more flexible and agile
- Be less prone to injuries

There are three ways to bring INTENSITY™ to your team:

1) **Get a team license** so that all your athletes can access the INTENSITY™ workouts at home and train in between cheer sessions. We offer yearly and monthly plans for teams of all sizes, so there is an option for all from just $20 per athlete per year.

2) **Book an INTENSITY™ Clinic** with one of our Master Trainers. At your clinic, our highly specialised staff will run fitness tests, teach you a warmup and conditioning routine to use all season, teach you some fun conditioning games, show athletes how they can maximise their skills by making the best out of their bodies and help clean/fix existing skills that your athletes find challenging.

3) **Get certified as an INTENSITY™ Coach** so that you can run classes for your athletes, parents, and friends to create a great additional revenue stream centred around cheerleading fitness.

CERTIFY AS AN INTENSITY™ COACH

Being a competitive cheerleader represents the top ability of the entire cheerleading world and being an athlete goes far beyond belonging to a competitive team. Dedication to ongoing physical and mental development is how true champions are made. In order to enhance performance and prevent injury, coaches need to have a thorough understanding of how the human body reacts to and performs athletic cheerleading activities.

What does it take to perform a cheerleading skill? It takes a combination of motor skills and strength. Most cheerleaders will spend hours working on perfecting their skill and almost no time to develop the specific muscles which make the skill great. If cheerleaders spent half as much time working on their fitness as they did on practicing their skill, it would take them half the time and aggravation to achieve their goals.

The Cheerobics® INTENSITY™ Coaching programme was designed to help coaches push athletes to the best of their abilities, develop their motor skills and maximise what their body is capable of.

Sessions and clinics are designed to be fast, effective, INTENSE and to help cheerleaders:

- ‣ Be leaner, faster, stronger
- ‣ Improve resistance of performing full out routines
- ‣ Drill & perfect techniques for jumping, tumbling, dance and stunting
- ‣ Be more flexible and agile
- ‣ Be less prone to injuries

The programme is designed to make better use of limited time, using every second of cheer training to its full potential. These objectives will be met by the coach's complete understanding of theoretical knowledge combined with physical ability to demonstrate and lead the workouts.

It is a myth that cheerleading practice alone will get you stronger and fitter. It is the structure of the practice and the amount of conditioning that will do so. Slow repetitions of a skill (with resting in between) are not going to strengthen your muscles. It is only going to use the strength you already have. Likewise, it is not the stunting that will make you fitter but the work that you do around it that will allow you to perform the stunt every time.

Whilst it is not realistic to get every team training like a Worlds team, ALL CHEERLEADERS can increase their performance and maximise their potential if they dedicate a bit more time to achieving greater fitness. A few adjustments to your training, your eating habits and your approach can transform your potential and turn you into the athlete you always wanted. It's time to turn up the intensity of your training with Cheerobics® INTENSITY™!

Made in the USA
Columbia, SC
25 May 2019